To:

From:

Message:

Published by Christian Art Publishers
PO Box 1599, Vereeniging, 1930, RSA

First edition 2022

Designed by Christian Art Publishers

Devotions taken from *Traveling Light* by Dalene Reyburn

Cover designed by Christian Art Publishers
Images used under license from Shutterstock.com

Set by Christian Art Publishers

Printed in China

ISBN 978-1-77637-174-7

22 23 24 25 26 27 28 29 30 31 – 10 9 8 7 6 5 4 3 2 1

A Journey of Joy

First things first

"Seek the Kingdom of God above all else, and live righteously, and He will give you everything you need." (Matt. 6:33 NLT)

Guaranteed peace comes from simply determining – each day – no matter what – to seek God first, first thing.

It's unbelievably uncomplicated. Difficult some days. But not complex. It's a matter of addressing your waking thoughts to Jesus. And don't let anyone throw shade because you're not a morning person who is energized by shiny-happy early encounters with God. (You're useful and astute when the morning people are heading for bed and the Kingdom needs all kinds of humans.) But as you surface from sleep and your thoughts gather coherence, just offer the day to God. Pray: Your Kingdom come; Your will be done.

As you move through the rushed minutes or the hours of waiting, keep up the appeal – Your Kingdom come; Your will be done. You may find it simplifies situations and distills decisions and amplifies God's answers like nothing else, and there's a new freedom to travel light.

God, You first; me second. Maximize my life today, for Your glory. Amen.

Already there

God saved you by His grace when you believed. And you can't take credit for this; it is a gift from God. (Eph. 2:8 NLT)

I am usually the first one up in the mornings to brew the coffee. But first an instinctive daybreak ritual unfolds. I unlock the kitchen door – and I stand there. I haven't gone anywhere or done anything yet. I'm just standing in the fresh air of a new day, and I just am.

That's how God's acceptance feels. We didn't earn or deserve it. God just receives us, delights in us, cherishes us, without us going anywhere or doing anything. It is as if we've made it. His acceptance rushes into our hearts like so much fresh morning air. And we can just stand there, and enjoy it.

For some, travel is about getting there. For others, it's about the journey. But what if you saw your life expedition as God does? From His eternal point of view, you've already arrived.

King of kings, there's no greater destination than Your courts! And I don't ever need to ask, "Are we there yet?" Amen.

Accepted and sustained

Jesus answered, "It is written: 'Man shall not live on bread alone, but on every word that comes from the mouth of God.'" (Matt. 4:4 NIV)

Jesus' relationship with His Father was marked by total acceptance. Matthew describes how, as Jesus was baptized, a voice said, "This is My dearly loved Son, who brings Me great joy" (Matt. 3:17). God accepted Him. There was more to their Father-Son relationship than just acceptance. There was sustenance.

Jesus spent regular, intimate time with His Father, drawing away to quiet places to pray (Luke 5:16). In John 4:34, He explains to His disciples, "My nourishment comes from doing the will of God, who sent Me." He lived in unbroken fellowship with the Father. God sustained Him.

In just the same way, the Father has entered into relationship with you – He accepts you. And He is growing and changing you – He sustains you. God satisfies your soul in ways nothing and no one else can.

Father God, please give me the spiritual sustenance, the emotional energy, the brain and body zest to do life well, and to Your glory. Amen.

Significant sojourner

Jesus grew in wisdom and in stature and in favor with God and all the people. (Luke 2:52 NLT)

Jesus lived with the calm, unshakeable conviction that He was accepted by His Father. So can we. Jesus lived knowing that His Father was the source of His sustenance. So can we.

And at just the right time, walking the dusty streets of ancient Israel, Jesus entered into remarkable, significant ministry. And so can we.

It seems God's game plan for Jesus on earth was thirty years of *preparation*, three years of impact. So if it feels to you as if your life isn't amounting to anything cosmically significant, remember that God's preparation of His Son was in and of itself cosmically significant. Don't underestimate how God is preparing you – and what He's preparing you for. *It's all significant.*

Jesus, I believe You accept me. I believe You sustain me. Help me trust that You're using me to make an indelible impact on this world, for Your Name's sake. Amen.

Right-side-up parenting

"Can a mother forget the baby at her breast and have no compassion on the child she has borne? Though she may forget, I will not forget you!" (Isa. 49:15 NIV)

I try to praise my children for the process not the product – rewarding for character not accomplishment. But I still sometimes catch myself parenting from achievement to acceptance, instead of from acceptance to achievement.

It's never wrong to affirm our kids. But moms, we're the voice in their heads. We're the soundtrack to the lives of our kids.

We need to be the lead vocalist, and the lyrics of the chorus that get stuck in their heads need to be: Win or lose, I love you. I love being your mom. I love watching you do your best with the gifts God's given you. If God had lined up all the children in the world and let me pick, I'd pick you every time.

You're accepted.

Good Father, help me parent my kids the way You parent me. Amen.

Don't be fooled

But the LORD said to Samuel, "The LORD doesn't see things the way you see them. People judge by outward appearance, but the LORD looks at the heart." (1 Sam. 16:7 NLT)

When Samuel goes to anoint David as king, Jesse parades his strapping older sons before Samuel. For each son Samuel thinks, "This must be the one?" And for each son God says, Nope. Finally Samuel asks Jesse if he doesn't have any other sons. Jesse calls for David and Samuel anoints him. And the rest is history.

As you focus on the truth that God accepts you – as is, without you doing, trying or being something bigger and better and more impressive or influential – would you remember that He doesn't see you as you see you? He doesn't take His cues from you.

Thankfully, His opinion of you isn't dependent on anyone else's opinion of you. It's also not dependent on your opinion of you. He sees you as you really are.

God, I'm so grateful You know me better than I know me, and still You love me. Amen.

Run and retell

The woman left her water jar beside the well and ran back to the village, telling everyone, "Come and see a man who told me everything I ever did! Could He possibly be the Messiah?" (John 4:28-29 NLT)

When this Samaritan woman encountered the astonishing grace and omniscience of the Savior, she ran back to her hometown to tell anyone who'd listen. We should be always running back to a remembrance and retelling of how God sees, knows and loves us utterly.

Don't worry about how He'll sustain you, or how He'll lead you into a life of significance, or how much you'll achieve for Him. All in good time. Just know that He knows everything about you – like He knew everything about the Samaritan woman. He hasn't taken His eyes off you for one second of your life. He's started something in you: a good work that He will complete (Phil. 1:6). It's the kind of good news that's worth remembering – and running to retell.

Jesus, I'm so happy to have encountered Your total knowing of me. It's mobilized me to make a difference. Amen.

Relationship before rules

"I am the LORD. I will free you from your oppression and will rescue you from your slavery in Egypt. I will claim you as My own people, and I will be your God." (Exod. 6:6-7 NLT)

God invites you into relationship with Him, as you are. He doesn't wait for you to prove yourself. He finds you in the middle of your mess and He says, I'll be your Dad.

God didn't give the Ten Commandments, then rescued the Israelites. He didn't say, "Ok, follow these ten rules and I'll consider your case. Maybe I'll be your God." He said, "I'll rescue you from Egypt. I'll split the sea for you. I'll be your God; you'll be My people. And now, because I love you – because I've set you free – live by this code. It'll bless and protect you."

Even before Jesus came to roll out the grace plan in our two-dimensional timeline, His Father was saving sinners by grace, through faith. It's always been relationship before rules.

Father, thank You for making the first move, even though I was playing hard to get. Amen.

Shadow selves

"Blessed are those who are invited to the wedding feast of the Lamb." (Rev. 19:9 NLT)

There isn't a Jesus-follower on the pages of history who hasn't been able to identify with Paul's struggle when he says, "I want to do what is good, but I don't. I don't want to do what is wrong, but I do it anyway" (Rom. 7:19).

It seems sometimes that we live with rogue tendrils of our temperaments – our shadow selves, as some call them. Even though Jesus Christ has invited us to a feast, our shadow selves are the bits we are embarrassed to bring with us. And yet Jesus sees all the bits of us – the ugly and the lovely parts of us.

Regardless of where we find ourselves on the sliding scale of sanctification – which is the part of salvation that happens between justification (repenting and committing to Christ) and glorification (our heaven-bound hope of total restoration) – He says, Come. Time at His table will bring our shadows into the light, to be dissipated by His love.

Jesus, thank You for inviting me –
all of me – to feast with You. Amen.

All the way

God has said, "I will never fail you. I will never abandon you." (Heb. 13:5 NLT)

Once, for Father's Day, our eldest son wrote a bunch of notes to my husband, Murray. He hid the notes all over the house and Murray would keep on coming across them randomly for weeks afterwards. Amongst the tea bags was scrawled: Dad, I wouldn't swap you for anything. Amidst his socks was, Dad, I think you're cool! By far the best one – buried in a breakfast cereal – said: Dad, thank you for never forgetting. (No pressure!)

Our Heavenly Father never forgets. He never stops watching us. He never stops walking with us. He never stops sending us reminders of His grace-grip on our lives. He sees the end from the beginning – and not a stretch of the journey takes Him by surprise.

Heavenly Father, thank You that
You're in this for the long haul.
Thank You for always
being with me. Amen.

Landmines

But You, Lord, are a shield around me, my glory,
the One who lifts my head high. (Ps. 3:3 NIV)

It seems the century we're standing in is one big anxiety minefield. It's as if every other person (maybe you and me?) is walking around with a ticking Improvised Explosive Device of the soul just waiting to go off when stepped on by others' Irritation, Embarrassment and Disappointment.

If we're honest, we're all somewhere on the anxiety spectrum. We need to diffuse our hearts from time to time before they get dangerous. And we need to help others do the same.

God has this to say about irritation, embarrassment and disappointment: He seeks you out and He rejoices over you with singing (Zeph. 3:17). The Father is not irritated. He entered time and space to get to you, and He advocates on your behalf (1 John 2:1). He's not embarrassed of you. You're the apple of His eye (Zech. 2:8). He's not disappointed in you.

Lord, thank You for going ahead of me to
clear the landmines. You are my safety and
the One who lifts my head high. Amen.

Gone guilt

He cancelled the record of the charges against us and took it away by nailing it to the cross. (Col. 2:14 NLT)

I would guess you're incredibly supple. You stretch your budget, schedule, patience and your caffeine threshold in superhero ways. You bend every which way to please and placate and catch whoever's falling. You love fiercely, and with a tender flexibility. And your psyche has plasticized so impressively that you can accommodate vast mental tracts of mom guilt, wife guilt, daughter guilt, friend guilt.

Except, women aren't superheroes. We're actual, human sinners. And God has dealt with your guilt – so, stop it already. He carried your shame. Why would you ask to carry something unbearably, impossibly heavy – something human arms can't ever stretch around – when Someone else has offered to carry it for you?

On days when you are guilty of sinning against others – for real – ask their forgiveness. Restore the relationship. Find each other again in the soft, strong circles of mercy. And move on, guilt gone.

Jesus, You were weighed down by my shame, so I could be set free. Amen.

Enough

While they are still talking about their
needs, I will go ahead and answer
their prayers! (Isa. 65:24 NLT)

Guilt tortures you with accusations that you're always behind on doing and being all you want to do and be. It nags that there's never enough time, never enough money, never enough you to go around.

There's enough time. There's enough time for the story you're living. But the chapter you're in is part of a much longer plot that climaxes in eternity. It's a beautiful, humbling thing to build something that will outlast you – something others will finish, to God's glory.

There's enough money. Guilt has you believing you're supposed to stretch your stressed out self over every gaping hole. That doesn't model dependency on God. It models delusional self-sufficiency. He knows your needs.

There's enough you. God makes sure there's fresh mercy every morning (Lam. 3:23). That means, it may feel like there's not enough you, but for sure there's enough grace for you not to give up.

God, You are enough, and You give
enough! Energize and mobilize
me with that truth. Amen.

14

Worth your wardrobe

I am overwhelmed with joy in the LORD my God! For He has dressed me with the clothing of salvation and draped me in a robe of righteousness. (Isa. 61:10 NLT)

For a school project on recycling, a friend's daughter made an outfit out of trash. She sewed together dried-out teabags and made an exquisite dress. What if we dressed ourselves, not in trash, but in the truth that we're wearing royal robes? That we're not so last season. We're so next season. So never-ending season. Because we're dressed for eternity.

We could sew together verses like so many teabags to remind ourselves and each other to dress like daughters – not orphans – because "God decided in advance to adopt us into His own family by bringing us to Himself through Jesus Christ" (Eph. 1:5). We might remember to carry ourselves as image-bearers of the Creator-King who sees us, knows us, and calls us chosen people, royal priests, a holy nation, God's very own possession.

Father, help me to remember who I am, and to dress accordingly. Amen.

Living eulogy

And you yourself must be an example to them by doing good works of every kind. Let everything you do reflect the integrity and seriousness of your teaching. Teach the truth so that your teaching can't be criticized. Then those who oppose us will be ashamed and have nothing bad to say about us. (Titus 2:7-8 NLT)

"Live so that the pastor says nice things about you at your funeral." This was genuine, well-meaning advice, offered to me as a teenager. It's a little crass maybe, and self-serving. But it can frame how we live – while we're living.

Let's decide to live well this year, so that we have brilliant stories to tell – and so that people coming after us have even better stories to live. Let's live well, not because we want recognition, but because we want to beat smooth paths for others to walk.

Lord, help me live each day
the way I'd want to tell it
to my grandkids. Amen.

Just information

"Don't be afraid," he said, "for you are very precious to God. Peace! Be encouraged! Be strong!" (Dan. 10:19 NLT)

A name on a travel document – even a photo – doesn't really tell you all that much about the person carrying it. It's evidence of who the person is – but it's not who the person is.

This is true for you too. Your identity is independent from – safeguarded against – any info thrust upon you. This is wonderful, powerful, very good news.

It is a great relief. Because if the information you receive is rejection or misunderstanding or misrepresentation – or if the info is that you're hoping to get invited or included or loved and you don't – that information will hurt and it will be difficult to process.

But it doesn't actually change anything about who you are, or your standing with the Heavenly Father. You're still utterly beloved. The rebuff or the nastiness – it's just information.

Lord, thank You that I don't have to qualify myself. You've already qualified me to be who You've called me to be, and all You've called me to be is myself. Amen.

Obedience over impact

For we will be counted as righteous when
we obey all the commands the Lord our
God has given us. (Deut. 6:25 NLT)

When we think of purpose, our minds might leap to fantasies of grand ideas and enormous influence. Except really, we'll be judged on our obedience, not our impact. God is pleased with our surrender to His will and His ways – more than He's pleased with the press we receive. You were created to make a difference, not an impression.

That's not to say you won't have grand ideas, or that God won't give you enormous influence. In fact, the more obedient you are, the more likely you are to have that kind of impact.

Dream your dreams. Set your goals. And know that true success is measured in daily, hourly, moment by moment obedience to your Heavenly Father.

God, You created purpose!
Help me only ever to look
for it in You. Amen.

18 *Immeasurable, untouchable*

Yours, O Lord, is the greatness, the power, the glory, the victory, and the majesty. We adore You as the one who is over all things. (1 Chron. 29:11 NLT)

Part of our purpose is healthy ignorance. Wholesome unawareness of how God is using His Spirit in us to bless others.

You will never know the impact you've had in this life. There's no accurate earthly glory-meter. You may catch glimpses of how God is making something beautiful from your life, but you'll only comprehend the sweeping scope of the stardust you've scattered when you view it from eternity.

And then, you won't be able to touch that glory, and you won't want to. You'll grasp with startling clarity that your life was never about your ambitions – your purposes. It was about God's purposes in and through you.

Creator God, would you send enough encouragement to keep wind in my sails – but please never send the gale force applause that will knock me off course. Your glory is the north star I'm sailing for. Amen.

Serious lightness

Be honest in your evaluation of yourselves, measuring yourselves by the faith God has given us. (Rom. 12:3 NLT)

We can all be reactionary extremists. Sometimes we're too flippant about what God has called us to. We don't appreciate the eternal urgency of the lives we lead on earth. We don't appreciate the seriousness of our sin: how it separates us from God, and how much He paid to close the gap. Other times we take ourselves far too seriously.

Part of discovering our purpose is learning to balance these extremes: carrying well the tension of not taking ourselves too seriously but simply being willing and available to be used by God as and when He chooses – and living passionately and excellently and with serious intent, for His glory.

What you're doing for God today was inked into God's plans from eternity past. It's a big deal! Concurrently, what you're doing for God today is just another brick in the Kingdom wall.

King of kings, help me never to take myself too seriously – even as I take You and Your ways very seriously indeed. Amen.

Irrefutably unseen

"My sheep listen to My voice; I know them, and they follow Me. I give them eternal life, and they will never perish. No one can snatch them away from Me." (John 10:27-28 NLT)

It's ok that others don't always recognize God's purposes in your life. The work He's doing in and through you won't always be evident to people around you. But there's a golden thread running through your existence, weaving your context and your character around the unique life's work that God has called you to. You're made in God's image and every day you're journeying more deeply into the likeness of Christ.

That reality will last forever, so it doesn't matter if your peeps don't see it or understand it. It's eternal. It is, because it is wrought in you by the great I Am.

Jesus, thank You that I don't need to be seen by the world when I'm seen by You. Amen.

Trained and equipped

You are a chosen people, a royal priesthood,
a holy nation, God's special possession, that you
may declare the praises of Him who called you out
of darkness into His wonderful light. (1 Pet. 2:9 NIV)

Peter was writing to Christians scattered across the Roman Empire. I'm pretty sure they didn't feel like a chosen people, a royal priesthood, a holy nation. They were being tortured for their faith. Despite their horrific circumstances, Peter reminded them of who they really were – of their royal purpose as God's chosen earthly ambassadors, and of how God had trained and equipped them for that role.

God doesn't call those who are qualified. He qualifies those He calls. We're not expected to labor until someone says we're good enough. God declares us good enough – then we work *from* approval, not *for* approval. He bestows on us fantastic credentials, even when things around us seem bleak, so we're fully equipped to spread His fame to a dark and desperate world.

God, remind me that I've already graduated.
Help me live each day as if I really believe the
things You've written on my résumé. Amen.

22 *The next step*

Commit everything you do to the LORD.
Trust Him, and He will help you ...
The LORD directs the steps of the godly.
He delights in every detail
of their lives (Ps. 37:5, 23 NLT).

What if we simply, habitually, prayed for God to give us His desires, each day, trusting Him to show us the next step? Wouldn't it make life astronomically simpler?

Start by praying: *God, what would please You?* He'll answer by finetuning the desires of your heart. He'll adjust your tone, your reactions, your choice of words, the current direction in which your decisions are taking you – if any of those things are dishonoring to Him.

The psalmist tells us that God delights in the details of our lives. He directs every step. Ask Him to lay His desires on your heart – then pay attention. What are you *passionate* about, and good at? Which ideas haven't gone away? Which situations or encounters clarify your values? How are you pressing on to take hold of that for which Christ Jesus took hold of you (Phil. 3:12)?

What's the next step, Lord? Amen.

Awareness

"The thief comes only to steal and kill and destroy. I came that they may have life and have it abundantly." (John 10:10 ESV)

When we take hold of the truth that we're entirely *accepted* by God – based on nothing we've done to deserve that acceptance but on His love and power alone – and when we've realized that Jesus came to bring us not just life but life in abundance and when we've gratefully received that life – we come into a whole new sense of being. A whole new awareness of identity.

Once you've owned who you are, and Whose you are, you'll be done striving for belonging and affirmation and purpose. You can get busy doing what God has called you to do. In fact, the what becomes clearer when you've settled the who. It all begins to add up.

Father, thank You that knowing who I am (Yours!) is so often the obvious and immediate clue to discovering what I should be doing with my life. Amen.

Noise

"Whoever belongs to God hears what God says ..." (John 8:47 NIV)

Train platform announcements and airport terminal last-calls are notoriously indecipherable. *"This is the final call for passenger hwah-hwah-hwah. Please board at Gate shweh-shweh ..."* The information we need most is often a blur of sound or static. Fathoming our purpose and hearing God's voice in a noisy world can feel just the same. I know I've definitely felt lost, alone and bewildered, and you probably have too.

Maybe the thing is to keep still for a bit. Anxiously – recklessly – running between boarding gates can heighten the hysteria and confusion. Keep from frantically asking, "Where am I now? Where have I landed? Where am I going? Where am I supposed to be?" Rather say, "Lord, I'm here. Find me." And trust that the ultimate tour guide and the most efficient airport security personnel officer – Jesus – will make His way through the throngs and do just that.

Good Shepherd, I have no idea where I am.
Please meet me right here, and take
me where I need to be. Amen.

Purpose precision

In His grace, God has given us different gifts for doing certain things well ... (Rom. 12:6 NLT)

As you commit to living out God's you-plan, ask Him to give you wisdom and clarity around your gifts. You're not doing yourself or the world a favor if you're delusional about what you can and can't do.

That said, He has gifted you uniquely and distinctively, and He has planned since eternity past where, when and how He'll use you: your sensitivity, your razor-sharp creativity, your scintillating personality, or whatever it is you have to offer the world. So ask Him to confirm where, when and how you can position yourself in sweet spots of maximum efficacy.

Next: ask God to help you recognize the lies of the enemy – limiting beliefs you've picked up. There will always be opposition to your purpose. It's one of the things that makes uncovering it a kind of daring quest.

Lord, You're a God of detail and specifics. You don't deal in generics. I trust You to protect me from contesters to my destiny, and to lead me into my precise purpose. Amen.

26 Purpose versus perfection

Now all glory to God, who is able, through His mighty power at work within us, to accomplish infinitely more than we might ask or think. (Eph. 3:20 NLT)

If you're a perfectionist (takes one to know one), please don't let yourself get in your own way to finding and fulfilling your purpose. Moses, Elijah, David, Rahab and a bunch of others – they were all flawed humans who offered all of their imperfect selves.

Living deep and wide into God's purposes for us – walking to the borders of our inheritance – welcoming the abundant life designed for us – all of that ushers in wondrous contentment and fulfillment. But to get to that most satisfying place, we're going to have to get over ourselves and our impossible personal standards. We're going to have to get over what others think of us.

We will always be broken vessels. But the Father is strong in us, able to do immeasurably more than we ask or think, and able to lead us into His purposes for our lives.

*God, this is all of imperfect me,
leaning into all of
Your perfect purpose. Amen.*

Final word

... for it is God who works in you to will and to act in order to fulfill His good purpose. (Phil. 2:13 NIV)

When you don't get the affirmation, affection, admiration or acceptance from others that you long for – the warm fuzzy feelings that (you think) will confirm your calling – you don't actually have the right to sulk, or doubt. Silence or rejection from others, or having your efforts disregarded or misconstrued – these are not necessarily indications of what is or isn't your purpose.

Other people's responses can be insightful, and even an indication of the direction we should pick. Just remember: you're fulfilling God's purpose in *your* life – not in the lives of the people commenting or criticizing. Have your trusted advisors who will tell you the truth, then go with your gut. Go with what you know God is prompting you to do. He drew up the plans for your life, and He gets to have the final word.

Jesus, keep me and anyone else from finishing Your sentences. When it comes to my purpose, please have the last say. Amen.

Purposeful failure

The godly may trip seven times, but they will get up again. But one disaster is enough to overthrow the wicked. (Prov. 24:16 NLT)

We all know failure is inevitable. More than that, failure is so often the path to your greatest success as a purpose-hunter.

The key to using failure as a means of moving forward in the present moment – as opposed to wallowing in the past, which helps no one – is to do a few don'ts. Don't ask, "Why me?" Don't look for sympathy and don't indefinitely keep on accepting condolences from others. Don't blame, and don't complain.

Even in the midst of horrid, embarrassing, egg-on-face failure, try to call to mind the truth that we have a hope that does not disappoint (Rom. 5:5), and we have a God who causes all things to work together for our good (Rom. 8:28). Even failure.

Father, thank You that I can offload the baggage of my mess-ups. Thank You that You will use even these failures to fulfill Your purposes for me. Amen.

Big picture

Where there is no vision, the people perish. (Prov. 29:18 KJV)

It's possible you're struggling to see a way forward. Perhaps you feel desperate, and strength-sapped. You can't quite see a way to launch yourself effectively into the riptides and rigors of real life.

Having a big picture perspective may give you the vision you need. Keep the big picture stuck up on the bathroom mirror of your mental landscape and glance at it every day.

Get perspective on where you are. For example, the parenting season you're in may feel unending and all-consuming. But very, very soon, it will be over. You have still got a huge chunk of life to live.

Get perspective on legacy. You're leaving one. Get perspective on your journey, and your kids' journeys. A decade or so from now, you're hoping they'll be confident, content grownups who love God and others. Pray big prayers and dream big dreams with that in mind.

Lord God, don't let me lose sight of the big picture, and my small place in the world, so I can keep perspective. Amen.

Small picture travel

They have made God's law their own, so they will never slip from His path. (Ps. 37:31 NLT)

Small picture travel is about proximity. *Nearness.* Small picture travel-through-time helps me remember, for example, that when my boys ask me to play soccer and I snap at them – *Not now!* – that's all they see. They see a small picture of what's happening in my day. They haven't just read the email with news that sent my head spinning. All they experience is the *Not now!* Sure, life happens and they'll learn that I can't always drop everything for soccer, but I want to get better at bending low and close, to explain that.

Small picture travel is deep-breath slow-down grace-for-today living. It is responding instead of reacting. This kind of travel is about routine and spontaneous non-routine, remembering that routine isn't boring; it's calming. And occasional change in routine isn't unsettling; it's stimulating. Noticing the little moments in each day will help us manage a healthy balance of both.

God, let the momentum of my small picture decisions steer my ship towards big picture shores. Amen.

Every masterpiece you meet

For we are God's masterpiece … (Eph. 2:10 NLT)

At bedtime one night, our eldest son (who is visually impaired), cried because his magnifier is too big for his school desk. Our youngest (who is not visually impaired) cried because he wishes he could also have fancy magnifiers to supersize his homework.

It's all *so unfair*, they said. I replied: *You can't blend in when you were born to stand out.* Every masterpiece is created to stand out. God calls *each one* of us His masterpiece. We all feel the pain of the chisel chipping away to make us beautiful. We feel the pain in different places, in different ways.

Plato said we should always be kind, because every person we meet – every masterpiece we meet – is fighting a hard battle. So here's to daily kindness to our kids, our colleagues, ourselves – as we allow the Master to do His wise work.

Maker of every masterpiece, make me brave
to stand out for You, however You choose
to display Your workmanship. Amen.

Meaning and magnitude

Instead, God chose things the world considers foolish in order to shame those who think they are wise. And He chose things that are powerless to shame those who are powerful. (1 Cor. 1:27 NLT)

What looks impressive to the world is not always impressive to God. And what looks insignificant and inconsequential to the world might be of staggering eternal value – or not. The difference hinges on the heart.

We can be simultaneously humbled and comforted by an understanding that, whether we're on a stage before thousands, or whether we're alone doing menial chores at home, in both scenarios we're wearing His royal robes. Both undertakings can and should be of equal eternal significance. Because we can and should be doing both with a heart bent on honoring only Him.

If we're doing what we do as a love offering to God – an act of worship with Him at the center and us on the periphery – then whether it's done before millions or only One, the impact and importance are eternal.

Father, help me purpose my every feat – viral or invisible – to magnify Your splendor. Amen.

Surrender

Now may the God of peace ... equip you with all you need for doing His will. (Heb. 13:20-21 NLT)

When we decide to hitch our destinies to Jesus – surrendering wholly to God – we surrender our ambitions too. We surrender our big ideas about our purpose. We choose to align our lives with *God's* purposes in and through us – happily letting go of what we think that should look like.

That all sounds easier than it really is. But if we really trust Him – if we believe He is who He says He is and that He loves us, protects us, never leaves us nor forsakes us – then we have to be ok to submit ourselves daily to His best plans and purposes. It's His Kingdom after all. He made us – and He made us His heirs. It makes sense that He would know better than us how best we can be used.

Father and Creator, I've got a bunch of pictures in my head of what I think You should do with my life. But I'm happy to go with Your designs. Amen.

Spit it out

Confess your sins to each other and pray for each other so that you may be healed. (James 5:16 NLT)

We'll never be operating in our full, fantastic purpose if there's unconfessed sin in our lives. And sin has a way of showing up, no matter how well we think we're hiding it. The people around you might not know exactly what's going on, but for sure they know something's going on. Hiding and hanging on to sin has us living with a limp.

Don't ever deceive yourself into thinking you don't need the checks and balances of authority and accountability to lead you into your purpose. The truth comes out – somewhere, somehow, sometime. Every time. Maybe it's wise to fear the consequences of concealment more than we fear the consequences of confession.

As difficult and awkward as confession will probably be, don't put it off for another day. Come clean. You'll be so grateful you did.

Father God, it's Your kindness that leads me to repentance. Give me the courage to confess my sin and the assurance of Your absolute absolution. Amen.

Purpose with humble pie

Not to us, O LORD, but to Your name goes all the glory for Your unfailing love and faithfulness. (Ps. 115:1 NLT)

When we make our endeavors all about ourselves, we'll either experience tremendous performance pressure and self-consciousness, or we'll be arrogant and self-centered. Either way, not pretty.

But adopting a not-about-me approach frees us to relish our purpose with ease because we're handing over any results or accolades to the God who initiated our purpose and set us up to walk in it. Our purpose is far more satisfying – and attractive – when we serve it with a slice of humble pie.

Humility always seems to usher in remarkable expressions of God's might and magnitude. His cosmic strength is available to us when we're willing to open our hearts and our hands, allow others to see our weaknesses, and admit that we need God to come through for us.

Father, forgive me for all the times I've allowed my purpose to go to my head. Keep me humbly, happily, depending on You to do in me and through me all that You've planned. Amen.

Knee time

Never stop praying. (1 Thess. 5:17 NLT)

If you're keen to figure out your purpose, there's no substitute for prayer.

Sometimes the circumstances will be telling you one thing but when you get on your knees, God says the opposite. I know that if I react to circumstances without quieting myself in prayer and waiting for the still small voice of the Father, I mess up.

Sometimes we also seek God's hand, when He longs for us to seek His face. We want to see Him act within our circumstances – we want Him to confirm our purpose in some tangible way – when He's inviting us into intimacy with Him so that we can hear His heart.

Don't put off time alone with the King even if you're a little bit afraid of what He might say. He only ever seeks your good and His glory. Trust Him. And let the words of Gene Edwards comfort you: 'Beginning empty handed and alone frightens the best of men. It also speaks volumes of just how sure they are that God is with them.'

Father, draw me into calm and constant conversations with You. Amen.

Comfort

God is our merciful Father and the source of all comfort. He comforts us in all our troubles so that we can comfort others. (2 Cor. 1:3-4 NLT)

The word *comfortable* doesn't mean at ease. It means stronger. Comfort doesn't say, *Oh you poor* thing! Comfort says, *You can do it!* Because the prefix *com* means *with*, and *fort* is from the Latin – *fortis* – meaning *strong*. So if you say to someone, *Can I comfort you?* You're saying, *Can I with-strong you?*

You know anything worthwhile in life – a good education, a great marriage – will cost you some time, effort and emotional resources. Things that come easy – low-barrier achievements – also come cheap. So if you're aiming for some high-barrier achievements listen for the voices saying, *I'm here for you! I know you can get it together and be extraordinary!*

Your kind and tender Heavenly Father is the source of all comfort and He offers you that comfort without reserve. But He's urging you not just to ease your pain, but rather to seek His strength.

God of all comfort – with-strong me!
Use me to with-strong others. Amen.

Small comfort

"Go with the strength you have, and
rescue Israel from the Midianites.
I am sending you!" (Judges 6:14 NLT)

When the angel of the Lord tells Gideon to defeat the Midianites, Gideon says, "No way; I'm such a loser!" The angel calls him "mighty hero" (Judges 6:12) – even though Gideon is a bit of loser at this point. Then the angel comforts Gideon, saying, "Go with the strength you have."

He doesn't say, "You've got lots of strength!" Because Gideon doesn't have lots of strength. But he's got a little bit. And he goes with that little bit of strength. He keeps on going with it. And he defeats the Midianites.

So there'll be days when you don't have lots of strength. *But you've got a little bit of strength.* Enough maybe to swing your legs over the bed. Flick on the coffee machine. Go with the strength you have. Keep going with it. Until you realize you've made it through the day after all.

God, here's the last bit of my strength.
Give me the courage to go with it. Amen.

Comfortable with discomfort

... Jesus instructed His disciples to have a boat ready so the crowd would not crush Him. He had healed many people that day, so all the sick people eagerly pushed forward to touch Him. (Mark 3:9-10 NLT)

It's tough to strike a balance between self-preservation and martyrdom. Culture tends to say, *Look out for Number One! You can't love others until you've loved yourself!* This insidious message creeps in through inspirational memes and friends who tell us what they know we want to hear. But it smacks of selfishness.

The opposite is what happens to people in churches, schools, non-profits and families: total burnout from giving themselves over to worthy causes at the expense of all reason and wisdom. Jesus got it right. He poured Himself out unreservedly for others. Then He rested. He never burned out. He knew that He needed boundaries and emergency escape boats, and He knew that love is seldom convenient. He lived well and wisely within that tension.

Jesus, show me when, where and how
to expend my time and energy,
generously and wisely. Amen.

A happy home

A wise woman builds her home, but a foolish woman tears it down with her own hands. (Prov. 14:1 NLT)

I hate crumbs. Sometimes my boys are still eating and I'm lifting their plates to wipe the kitchen table. The world needs tidy people and laissez-faire people, which is why God created both kinds of human and mostly gets us to marry each other.

Wherever *you* find yourself on the home front, trust God to transform you, making you the maker of a home that's (mostly) clean and neat. Beautiful, within the bounds of practicality and imperfection. Doors wide open to anyone He brings.

Know that when you're dead and gone, you won't want your kids to reminisce, "Mom always dusted the piano keys! We grew up clean!" But rather, "Mom let us bang out any old wild and tuneless composition. We grew up free." Let's make sure people know that under our roof there's good coffee, good conversation and comfort. That courage and compassion are valued more than clean counters.

Father, help me remember that mess is sometimes just a sign of life, because people live here. Amen.

Travel mates

I am my lover's, and my lover is mine ... (Song 6:3 NLT)

Marriage is a long, beautiful road to walk, and you will want to be strong enough – and as comfortable as possible – for the journey. Get comfortable by living well the tension of complementing each other: filling up with your strengths the gaps created by his weaknesses while never enabling him by constantly covering his tracks.

To know the difference between comfort and codependence, in any given situation, ask yourself: *Do I need to call him out on this thing, because he's better than this and I have the inside track on his life and if I don't hold him accountable, who will? Or, is it that he's just not particularly organized and it helps him if I get stuck in to help?*

To travel far and comfortably in marriage, regularly replenish your own soul. Restore healthy respect for your husband and relinquish inappropriate control. You're not reducing yourself – just loving your man humbly, as you'd expect him to love you.

Jesus, I pray we'd make each other better
and better versions of ourselves. Amen.

Comfortable exclusivity

Know that the LORD has set apart His faithful servant for Himself; the LORD hears when I call to Him. (Ps. 4:3 NIV)

The word holy means cut out of a template. Framed for a specific *purpose*. It means *different* or *distinguished* or *distinct* from. It means set apart. Setting ourselves apart – aligning our lives with Jesus because of how He drew us close – that makes us holy, even though we're still wholly damaged and deficient.

Whether or not you get it all right all the time as a wife, you're still a *holy* wife, because you're set apart exclusively for your man. No shame in that. And whether or not you get it all right all the time as a mom, friend, boss, co-worker or volunteer team member, if you're called to those roles, then God has set you apart to fulfill them as part of your life's work and you can steward and enjoy them as holy tasks.

Lord God, strengthen me to do the things You've set me apart to do, and do them well. Amen.

Comfortable kindness

Be kind to each other, tenderhearted, forgiving one another, just as God through Christ has forgiven you. (Eph. 4:32 NLT)

I've asked my boys about the best girls in their class at school – the nicest girls. I ask them, "What makes her the best girl?" The answer is not, "She's so pretty," or "She's so smart," or "She's so thin," or "She's so *together*". The answer, without fail, is: "She's so kind."

Researchers into what your husband really wants from you have uncovered that, shockingly, he doesn't want you to iron his socks or fetch his slippers. He doesn't want a maid or a golden retriever. Really, he just wants you to be nice to him, and nice to the kids.

Your husband married his best friend. His girlfriend. You. Try not to hide behind the crazy and the kids. Try letting the to-do list get a little longer, and just be that girl.

Father, help me to keep
a soft heart towards my man.
Give me fantastic ideas of
ways I can show pure,
unadulterated kindness,
every day. Amen.

Not done yet

And I am certain that God, who began the good work within you, will continue His work until it is finally finished on the day when Christ Jesus returns. (Phil. 1:6 NLT)

You might have heard people tell you their marriage is over. You might have said it yourself.

Please don't give the enemy an inch. Please – before you give up on your marriage – turn your eyes to the future. Love who your spouse is becoming. Paul assured the Philippians that God wasn't done, and that He would certainly finish what He was busy with in their lives. You're not perfect and neither is your spouse. But one day – yay! – all flaws and weird idiosyncrasies will be ironed out glorious because God has perfection planned for you both and how cool is that?

Do another day of life with your lover, knowing it marks a little more passing of the old. A little more ushering in of the new. A little more Jesus.

God, help me remember that I'm not all I should be – not all I will be – and neither is my man. Amen.

Happiness

... for each one should carry their own load. (Gal. 6:5 NIV)

If your kids are still living at home, you'll know you're on the cusp of this one short parental season to love and lead them well.

Let's determine to grow kids who know that we love them. But that *they are responsible for their happiness.*

They hold their own happy and they need to be sure they're not handing it around expecting others to hold it for them. It's too heavy – too unfair – to expect anyone else to haul it about and hand it back gift-wrapped.

That said, let's try to be fun to live with. Let's find adventure. Wrestle entitlement to the ground and grin our victory in grateful, simple thanks. Let's pick experiences over things, character over comfort, and relationships over pretty much everything. Let's choose our own happy, hold onto it, and encourage our kids to do the same.

God, keep me from moping and blaming my misery on others. Help me carry the happy load of my own contentment, inspiring those around me to do the same. Amen.

Decision comfort

Yes, each of us will give a personal
account to God. (Rom. 14:12 NLT)

Children need to know they are responsible for their decisions. Depending on how big your kids are, you may need to do your fair share of handholding for a while yet. But ultimately, it's all up to them.

It's up to us, however, to model integrity. Let's help them hear God's voice above the din of culture. Let's show them how to dig for truth beneath lies and assumptions. And at every twist and dip and hurdle and cliff, let's commit to calling out courage and wisdom from their supple, strengthening hearts. I suspect it's going to get harder before it gets easier.

I suspect that we will wonder every other day if parenting is supposed to be this hard. I suspect we are choosing the path of maximum resistance, and maximum reward. But I suspect we will all survive, and be so very glad.

Jesus, I hope and pray my kids and I
will be firm friends on the far side of
these parenting paths. Amen.

Over and over comfort

"The Comforter, which is the Holy Ghost, whom the Father will send in My name, He shall teach you all things, and bring all things to your remembrance, whatsoever I have said unto you." (John 14:26 KJV)

Some of the best parenting advice we were ever given was, *Figure out what your kids need to hear from you, in order to be shaped by acceptance, not rejection. Then, tell them ten times more than you think they need to hear it.*

Depending on age, stage of life and temperament, our kids all need to hear different things. But your list might include:

God loves you. God gifted you. God forgives you, and never forgets about you. God's plan for you is the best plan for you. You're brave and beautiful; handsome and smart. You have what it takes. You've worked so hard. I love you no matter what. I love spending time with you. I'm listening. I'm proud of you. I trust you to plan and pray.

God, help me live, love and parent
so my kids never doubt Your comfort
and acceptance, or mine. Amen.

Doing family

Children are a gift from the LORD; they are a reward from Him. (Ps. 127:3 NLT)

No matter what kind of a family you were part of growing up – and what kind of a family you're part of now – "familying" can feel like traveling nowhere slowly.

To family means to do the over-and-over of slowly getting somewhere. We *family* when we keep on making and remaking circles of mercy. When we keep on finding each other – forgiving each other – no matter how many times we've been annoyed or disillusioned. We family with the satisfaction that each time we circle back to ordinary moments, by God's grace we know and love each other a little more.

When we *start* a family, we have no idea how to *finish* a family well. All we can really do is family in the now by keeping on choosing brave over easy, remembering that there is always hope.

God, make our home calm, welcoming, warm and safe – a refuge for rest and wrestling where we can learn well how to family. Amen.

Friend zones

"But I say, love your enemies! Pray for those who persecute you!" (Matt. 5:44 NLT)

There's a time to travel in circles – to walk the same ways, wearing smooth relational paths of trust and comfort. And there's a time to walk the hard ground of discomfort where stones get in your shoes or you stub your toes, because sometimes we need to walk towards the people who irritate and offend us. The people who disagree with us, or who just *dis* us in general.

It may be time to be honest with ourselves about comfortable friend zones – admitting that the reason we won't step out of those zones or away from those zones, is fear. It can be terrifying to travel towards someone who is different from us or who threatens our sense of safety in some other way. But sometimes, taking a step towards the thing that scares us most is what changes the world.

Father God, help me see humans – not hostility. Help me see potential friends instead of likely foes. No matter how scary or uncomfortable things get, help me to love anyway. Amen.

Comfy-pants friends

You were cleansed from your sins when you obeyed the truth, so now you must show sincere love to each other as brothers and sisters. Love each other deeply with all your heart. (1 Pet. 1:22 NLT)

Lots of grownups haven't got friendship totally figured out. Millions of words have been bled into best-selling books about friendship. That speaks of a gap in the market, and maybe a crisis of culture.

Self-preservation is a global epidemic. At the same time, social media tramples walls, connecting us vast and shallow to thousands of people, and leaving us lonelier than ever.

Despite our flurries of activity and achievement, we're increasingly insular, and uncomfortable. Instead of being our imperfect, stretchy-pants selves, we squeeze into trendy skinny-jeans friendships that look good or impress others. We get hurt – and hurt others – when we dress up our friendships in what isn't completely honest, or comfortable, or true to ourselves. Let's be better than that: creating safe, breathable, lasting friendships.

Friend of friends, help me accurately assess my friendships: what I've loved and appreciated, what's helped and hurt. Amen.

Treading heights

He makes me as surefooted as a deer, enabling me to stand on mountain heights. (Ps. 18:33 NLT)

Whether you're a high-earner or an only-just-survivor, you'll need to challenge culture's lie that you live and then you die, and it would be cool to be comfortable in between.

Ask God to give you renewed excitement to create opportunities for a growing generation – a fresh vision of the future you're shaping and the legacy you're leaving.

And try to see yourself the way God sees you: a fortress of integrity, protection and provision for those He's placed in your care. In the worry and drudgery of too much month at the end of the money, don't lose your sense of wonder or sense of humor. Be assured the Sovereign Lord is your strength, making you as surefooted as a deer, able to tread upon the heights.

God, lift the shroud of pressure and panic. Give me Your mantle of peace and perspective. Settle my soul with Spirit-level equilibrium – so that deep beneath surface noise and melee, I'd be quiet. Content. Unshaken. Amen.

52

Attitude of acceptance

Encourage each other and build each other up, just as you are already doing. (1 Thess. 5:11 NLT)

As you seek to comfort and be comforted by your people, allow *attitude* and *acceptance* to inform more of your thinking – at home, at work, with your husband, your best friend or your mom-in-law. Because in every relationship – from inner circle besties to casual acquaintances – we're either focusing on someone's good qualities, or their bad qualities. Acceptance of others' failings, and an attitude realignment towards their fortes, could set those relationships on new and astonishing trajectories.

Also, if you're a Highly Sensitive Person (that's me), then you tend to take responsibility for other people's happiness. You internalize conflict. You over-analyze, trying to solve people. But, God places us in relationships, not so we can change others, but so He can change us into more of Him. It's up to us to be Jesus to them – so that when they bump up against us they find themselves in a place of peace.

Jesus, please give me Your attitude towards people, and help me accept them the way You do. Amen.

Comfortable to overcome

But thanks be to God! He gives us the victory through our Lord Jesus Christ. (1 Cor. 15:57 NIV)

Overcomers give more than they get. They know that celebrating how someone else's light shines doesn't dim their own; it just showcases their generosity, humility and untarnished love. Overcomers celebrate others to pre-empt the jealousy, self-pity or disappointment they'll feel if they rely on circumstances to go their way. By giving more than they get, they make their own happy.

Overcomers don't give in; they get comfortable. An old overcomer's prayer reads: *The longer I walk with You, Lord, I find I have no enemies: only Your gift of chisels etching me deep.*

Overcomers aren't shocked and offended by failure, exhaustion and setbacks. They learn to befriend their menacing mentors. They stop fearing change and growth. They get comfortable with discomfort. Mostly, overcomers get comfortable in the arms of the Savior who suffered – and overcame.

Jesus, thank You for overcoming death,
so I can be an overcomer – in
this life and the next. Amen.

Sent

I have chosen to be faithful; I have determined to live by Your regulations. (Ps. 119:30 NLT)

Part of being willing to pilgrim through life for God – traveling through time on His terms – is answering His call wherever we are and going wherever He sends.

That sounds exciting! Or not. Because the call to travel into days of obedience won't necessarily be glamorous. (Like, I might be picturing a leisure estate with a sea view – and God might call me to a seedy highway motel). But wherever He leads us in our days on earth, His grace will be new every morning, and enough to sustain us in whatever He's called us to do and be (Lam. 3:22-23, 2 Cor. 12:9).

Plus, we always have the comfort of prayer. So let's pray. Let's pray until it engages our emotions. Let's be brave to look at the glamorous and the unglamorous parts of ourselves in light of prayer.

Jesus, whether the scenery is boring or beautiful, I want to go wherever You send me. Amen.

Brilliant view

"For just as the heavens are higher than the earth, so My ways are higher than your ways and My thoughts higher than your thoughts." (Isa. 55:9 NLT)

Sometimes we think God should put us up in the Ritz, and instead He has us rolling out our sleeping bags on the gravel. It's hard and cold. Uncomfortable. Unpleasant. Where's the rescue He promised?

But then maybe you look up. And it's just oh my gosh ... The boundless brilliance of a million stars glinting above you in the ink of night. If God had booked you into the Ritz you would have completely missed out on the vaulting luminosity of His cosmos.

It's in second-choice places of disturbance, discomfort and pain that we see the intensity of God's love and presence – His person and His purposes – most clearly. Get yourself a great sleeping bag and get ready to roll it out under any lovely sky of His choosing.

Father, thank You for only allowing pain to slip through Your fingers so that it can fall on me like stardust, displaying Your splendor. Amen.

Routine and non-routine

God created everything through Him, and nothing was created except through Him. The Word gave life to everything that was created, and His life brought light to everyone. (John 1:3-4 NLT)

Routine is essential for making the world go round. Without routine, things fall apart. And yet a break from routine – a spontaneous change in the rhythm of the humdrum – sparks life in beautiful ways. So, routine is always the springboard for spontaneity. Without routine, so-called spontaneity would just be random. Without routine, haphazard happenings would just be instability and unpredictability.

Routine, and non-routine, are essential for marriage, parenting, work, leisure, food and friendship. It's ok to embrace both. Because there's something settling and satisfying about having dinner on the table at the same time every night – and there's something marvelous and magical about sometimes eating it in a tent in the garden. Let's make space for both.

Jesus, show me how to live well, so that I'm not erratic or dangerously unpredictable, but happy to seize moments, and lighten up. Amen.

Coram Deo

You will show me the way of life, granting me the joy of Your presence and the pleasures of living with You forever. (Ps. 16:11 NLT)

Carpe diem – seize the day – is about making the most of every opportunity and living an extraordinary life. But sometimes in seizing the day – catapulting ourselves into all that we crave – we sacrifice wisdom on the altar of desire. There's an even more beautiful concept: *coram Deo*. It means *in the presence of God* and it protects the trajectory of our lives by steering us towards wisdom rather than hedonism, adrenalin or a need to prove ourselves.

Chara Donahue shares: "Carpe diem screams, 'Chase pleasure! Follow the flesh.' This eventually yielded heavy fruits of internal disharmony, confusion, and a constant lust for more. Living in the face of God, living *coram Deo,* is where I learned to lay hold of wisdom. Soon the fruit of the Spirit, true peace, true joy, and true love, were what emerged from my life."

God, earth-side, YOLO is a real thing. Help me live fully! But remind me to live always in Your presence, where I'll really live forever. Amen.

Go be still

For to me, living means living for Christ,
and dying is even better. But if I live, I can
do more fruitful work for Christ. So I really
don't know which is better. (Phil. 1:21-22 NLT)

One of the tough things about being human is that we are spiritual beings trapped in very unspiritual bodies. We're dust-to-dust flesh-and-blood growing older by the day – yet we know there's more to life, and more to come. We know that what we do on earth matters in eternity, and we look forward to total renewal and restoration. We are body-bound and heaven-spun.

We need to be acutely aware of the Big Picture – patiently waiting for it to unfold timeously and gloriously – so that we'll act immediately and obediently in the Small Picture – doing with urgency all we can within our circles of influence, to make a Kingdom difference. As we go and make disciples (Matt. 28:19), we're simultaneously still: knowing that He is God (Ps. 46:10).

Lord God, with You, all things are possible.
Ready me for Your purposes, even as
I rest in Your promise. Amen.

Huge God, tiny me

For the LORD your God is the God of gods and Lord of lords. He is the great God, the mighty and awesome God. (Deut. 10:17 NLT)

I easily fall into the trap of making my own plans, living my own life, doing it my way, and being in control. So God often needs to remind me of His enormousness. He needs to take me to the end of myself – where real life begins. Because at the end of my very small self I get to a spectacular, panoramic view of a world which is all about living for Him, and others.

Making big plans to fashion a tiny little life wrapped around just me – isn't big at all. Let's be glad we serve an immeasurable God – closer than breathing yet spanning the stars and all eternity.

Let's be glad that He and His ways are wholly beyond our comprehension, let alone our control.

Almighty God, I'll never see Your bookends because You have none. I stand in awe of Your unfathomable, unreachable greatness and I can't believe Your power lives in me. Thank You! Amen.

Are you game?

Prepare your minds for action, keep sober in spirit, fix your hope completely on the grace to be brought to you at the revelation of Jesus Christ. (1 Pet. 1:13 NASB)

Whether you're bookish and indoorsy or energetic and outdoorsy – you need a spirit of adventure for the Kingdom work God has set you up to do.

Encouraging every mom, Sunday school teacher and God-follower, Jack Klumpenhower writes, "Jesus tells us that the work of proclaiming God's Kingdom is dangerous. It takes courage. It demands earnest prayer. It's more about faith than giftedness, and it requires no resources other than those God provides. It's a highstakes spiritual battle, using supernatural weapons. Anyone willing to engage the fight on this level is needed for the cause. Such an adventurer will reap a rare mix of power, humility, and wide-eyed joy."

Don't shy away from the grand venture of saying yes to a cause so much bigger than you.

Jesus, make me brave and keen to say yes to any operation You launch! I want to get on my game face, for Your Kingdom and Your glory. Amen.

Unboxed

It is for freedom that Christ has set us free.
Stand firm, then, and do not let yourselves be
burdened again by a yoke of slavery. (Gal. 5:1 NIV)

Maybe you've been boxed? Or maybe you've tried to box others – like your kids or your husband, your friends or employees? Mostly we box to feel in control (of our own insecurities).

I don't believe God is in the box business. In nature, things that get boxed – in eggs, wombs, cocoons – are only there for a season – and then they come out, and really live. God is all about freedom. And maybe it's good to recognize that we and others are made uniquely. God made us diverse to demonstrate that there's freedom in following a strong Savior who was anything but conventional.

No one flourishes under the iron fist of a control freak. Also, no one flourishes under the weirdness of superfluous, over-the-top, out-of-whack praise. Let's encourage instead of criticizing and affirm instead of inflating unrealistically. That feels more like freedom, yes?

God, I want my life to reflect, in every way,
that You've set me free. Amen.

Fear-free zone

Christ has set us free to live a free life.
So take your stand! Never again let anyone
put a harness of slavery on you. (Gal. 5:1 MSG)

If you're brave enough today, ask yourself what it is that's enslaving you. What's keeping you from venturing forth – looking up and out – marveling at the stars above you and the possibilities ahead? Christ set you free to live a free life. Are you living it?

Mostly, we're ensnared by insidious, vice-like fear, not so? Maybe your heart's pinned down by fear of the future. Maybe you fear for your personal safety, or you fear people's opinions. Maybe you fear the pressure to perform. Or perhaps you've forgotten you're actually free from the crippling power of sin.

Get help. Talk to someone. Enlist people to pray for you. Fear is not the boss of you anymore. Neither is sin, and neither is anyone else or their opinions. Only Jesus holds that rank in your life. And He has set you free.

Lord Jesus, remind me every hour of today that, like the song says, I'm free, free, forever, amen!

Wonder

May the God of hope fill you with all joy
and peace as you trust in Him, so that you
may overflow with hope by the power of
the Holy Spirit. (Rom. 15:13 NIV)

The first time I slept outside for a whole night, I was twelve, and freezing. The ground was stony but it was absolutely exhilarating. The great starry silence above awoke fresh wonder in me.

We don't need to sleep under the stars every night to sustain our sense of wonder. But we need to be sure we never lose it. And one way of guaranteeing we don't is to lean into what renders others wonder-struck.

When he was little, our youngest son was passionate about zebras. So I collected zebra photos wherever I went. The greatest reward was hearing my boy thanking Jesus at bedtime 'for all the zebras in our day'.

Whether it's zebras or today's lunch in a zip lock bag – there's wonder right now, right where you are.

Creator God, give me eyes to see
the stripes and strands of wonder You weave
into all of life, all the time. Amen.

Quench

Rejoice in our confident hope. Be patient in trouble, and keep on praying. (Rom. 12:12 NLT)

Enthusiasm is so often the mark of an extraordinary life. Because that word – enthusiasm – comes from the Greek word *entheos*, which means *God within*.

But there are those on earth and elsewhere who don't want to see God's Kingdom come. The enemy of our souls doesn't want our lives to flourish. He doesn't want our enthusiasm – the thrill of God-in-us – to spill over onto the parched ground of a wretched, desperate world.

Yet that's exactly what God's called us to do. We're called to be the tall glass of something cold for withered, unwatered souls. It will take courage and commitment, but we simply can't allow the cynics and the snide remarks to embezzle our joy. Ask God for wise ways to go on the flood offensive – inundating the dry spaces you fill with undeniable, unignorable joy.

God, fill me to the brim and keep on filling, so that Your love quenches those whose thirst has made them scornful and skeptical. Amen.

Abundance in the dust

We can rejoice, too, when we run into problems and trials, for we know that they help us develop endurance. (Rom. 5:3 NLT)

One year we went game viewing in the wilderness during a devastating drought. Even though much of the game had perished in the waterless heat, we had the privilege of more sightings than ever before. There was no long grass for the animals to hide behind. And they were all on the move in search of water.

When life is uncomfortable and difficult and we're tramping through parched land – it's often then that we see God's abundant blessings. Because when life is stripped of the trappings of plenty and ease, we see the hand of God. We even see His face.

When life is fat with prosperity, the ample goodness of the Lord is all around us, all the time, and yet somehow, we don't notice. It takes opening our eyes wide and honest in a place of need, to clear our vision.

Heavenly Father, You're so kind. Thank You for compelling me to seek You and find You. Amen.

Inflexibly flexible

"Walk with Me and work with Me – watch how I do it. Learn the unforced rhythms of grace." (Matt. 11:29 MSG)

When you get out of your comfort zone and into an adventure zone, it recalibrates the soul for simplicity and flexibility. It reminds us that we need to be absolutely inflexible on the important stuff, and absolutely flexible on absolutely everything else.

As Jesus-followers, we need to prioritize relationships, inflexibly. Life is too short to do anything but love people, and love God. And we dare not budge from the perspective we get, on His magnitude, when we're barefoot beneath stars and sun.

But, we need to be flexible about how our coffee is brewed. Flexible about the kids making a fort in the lounge with every single piece of bedding in the house.

Some days, it's ok to be flexible and allow weather or whim to dictate the rhythm of the day. Consider allowing yourself, today, the flexibility to experience the freedom of unbridled happiness.

Jesus, help me to be inflexible in my resolve
to be more flexible, simply embracing
the adventure around me. Amen.

Be wise under the skies

... make the most of every opportunity. (Col. 4:5 NIV)

Before you step into the adventure of today, be still. Breathe. You need to be strong to find common ground with others, and to dig into your capacity for creativity and decisions.

Be slow. Slow to empty out all your words on another. Slow to uncage your rage when things don't roll how you hoped. Wait. Be sure your response is the cure not the cause.

Be quick. Quick to give and forgive. Quick to listen wide open and soft to the hearts of others. Quick to offer your help, your seat, your sandwich, your suggestion or solution.

Be careful. You can say anything. Ask anything. Tact, timing and tone are key.

Be free. God has already paid your life's ransom. Which means, don't get trapped in tangles of unwise choices. Rather, obey. Not to earn God's favor or anyone else's, and not because obedience is the gravy train to success. Obey because that is success, and simple freedom.

God, give me all the wisdom I'll need
for today's adventure. Amen.

Brave heart

"I knew you before I formed you in your mother's womb. Before you were born I set you apart and appointed you as My prophet to the nations." (Jer. 1:5 NLT)

David said to Goliath, "You come to me with sword, spear, and javelin, but I come to you in the name of the LORD of Heaven's Armies" (1 Sam. 17:45). David wasn't outsized, out-speared or outsmarted, because he knew that no one could outdo his God. You, too, can be brave to step into big tomorrows, because the tomorrows come one at a time and you'll meet a big God in each one.

And in your courage, be kind. Live outside your skin enough to know what the world feels like coming up against someone else's. Be prepared to pray hero prayers. And be you. Of the seven billion people on earth, you only get to be one of them. Do the best you can at being the only you. He calls out the stars by name. He'll call out the treasures He's placed in you.

God, please kit me out for
kindness and courage. Amen.

Not what I pictured

Consider it pure joy, my brothers and sisters,
whenever you face trials of many kinds,
because you know that the testing of your faith
produces perseverance. (James 1:2-3 NIV)

Sometimes we have a picture of how we should behave and how life should work out as a result. We memorize Scripture – and so we should. We might read the best books and apply them practically – and it's a brilliant idea to do that.

And yet if you've lived a bit, you'll know that spiritual maturity isn't gauged and appraised on perfect behavior; it's measured in terms of persevering faith. No amount of intellectual know-how can plough the heartland that produces a crop of righteousness and stalwart devotion. It's the onslaught of life in all its beauty and hardship – and it's your response of faith, and more faith, and continued faith time and again up and down steep and slippery slopes – that results in robust reliance on our great God.

Father, things aren't going as I planned.
Help me trust that though this is not what I pictured,
You're producing in me something better. Amen.

Feel all the feelings

Rejoice in the Lord always. I will say
it again: Rejoice! (Phil. 4:4 NIV)

Considering the desperate state of the globe, more than ever we need to feel irrefutable truth. We need to notice and glory in the beauty of lights, food and music and every other good gift: the multi-sensory here-and-now reminders of the extravagant wealth God ushered into our poverty – the radiance He shone into our darkness.

We need to feel relief and gratitude that truth is always the perfect plumb line between the pendulum extremes of liberal and conservative. Let's be so steeped in truth that we wouldn't swing to the side of all things insubstantial, feel-good, flaky and fake.

Let's be so steeped in truth that we wouldn't swing to the side of all things Spiritless, straight-jacketed, law-bound and unadventurous. Because then, the truth, the whole truth and nothing but the gospel truth will produce in us well-founded, wild emotion. It will burst our hearts with joy. Flood our lives with peace.

Jesus, where I've grown bored and blasé –
shake me awake! I stand in awe of You! Amen.

Who are you (not)?

The One who calls you is faithful, and
He will do it. (1 Thess. 5:24 NIV)

Maybe what keeps you from living adventurously – from being and doing all God's called you to be and do – is the fear of being found out. There's a voice that says things like, *You're not who they think you are. You can't really do what you say you'll do.*

That voice is the sound of the very real fear that maybe you're not all you're cracked up to be. Yes, you're a weak, broken human with flaws and a fickle heart and yes, you're too easily swayed by pride and fear and a host of other sins. Me too. We're great sinners – but we rest in the gracegrip of a greater Savior.

He's bigger than your faults and your feelings of inadequacy. He's big *in* you and *through* you. In fact His bigness is manifested most beautifully when we authentically lean on Him in our weakness.

God, the calling You've placed on my life
sometimes scares me. Help me to trust
You every step I take. Amen.

What's your title?

... to them I will give within My temple and its walls a memorial and a name better than sons and daughters; I will give them an everlasting name that will endure forever. (Isa. 56:5 NIV)

Maybe if you knew your title – really knew it – it wouldn't matter who else in the world knew it or didn't know it – respected it or discarded it. You might know what it feels like to be the most important person in a room.

You might be a CEO, a member of Congress, a PhD or the President. Yet the greatest title that can ever and will ever be draped gloriously over your life is Child of God. And the extraordinary thing about that title is that it was a gift. You couldn't slave for it or buy it.

Knowing your title doesn't lead to arrogance or complacency or compromise, but to life-changing hope. And knowing your title will give you the confidence to follow Jesus on any adventure.

Jesus, thank You for rebuilding my reputation.
I'm excited to be exactly who
You say I am. Amen.

Call it what it is

If we claim we have no sin, we are only fooling ourselves and not living in the truth. (1 John 1:8 NLT)

Looking up to our great God leaves our sin no place to hide – though hiding it is exactly what we too often try to do. Not only is this ridiculous, and futile, but we're also committing spiritual malpractice by not calling it what it is: sin.

Loads of us are keen to change the world, yet we're unwilling for God to change us. More than anything we need to stand still under God's bigness and allow Him to heal our souls.

This is not a quick fix, but it's so worth doing. Because if there's a discrepancy between our inner world (what's really going on in our hearts) and our outer world (the way we project or perform or pretend), our whole world will cave in.

Holy God, who am I kidding? Keep me honest about my sin: naming it, so we can nuke it. Amen.

Look up. Look back.

You hem me in behind and before, and You lay Your hand upon me. (Ps. 139:5 NIV)

An all-encompassing panorama of the stars above helps with viewpoint. In looking up, we're somehow better able to look back and remember all God has done for us. Just as He's keeping the stars suspended and planets circling, He's ceaselessly doing enormous things in the background of your life, without you even realizing it.

There's also nothing like stars to remind you of the majesty of God – to remind you that He's greater and more powerful than anything you face. The God who hems you in behind and before is always bigger than any giant pacing on the peripheries.

What your Savior did for you is always bigger than whatever has been done to you. And He's not done displaying His brilliance through the stars, and you.

Savior and star-maker, remind me to look up –
to regain perspective on Your majesty.
And remind me to look back –
in awe of what You've done. Amen.

Hands-free

By His divine power, God has given us everything we need for living a godly life. (2 Pet. 1:3 NLT)

Handbags are necessary, but I wish they weren't. I love being hands-free, with no stuff to lug. When my boys were babies I made sure I had a backpack for a diaper bag. I didn't want to have a kid draped over one shoulder and a bag slung over the other. Even now, if my outfit has enough pockets for phone, keys and emergency headache pills? Brilliant.

There's something splendid about being spiritually hands-free too. And we can be. Jesus came to give us abundant life – spilling-over, filling-up, too-much-to-fit life. If we remember that we are so filled up with Him that we have all we need, we won't need to cart extra baggage. We can let go of cases laden with issues, because we carry within us the glorious fullness of sufficient life.

Lord, teach me how to collect and carry life's precious souvenirs. But keep me from carrying more than I categorically have to. Keep me hands-free – kitted out completely with all I need for life. Amen.

Maximize

Jesus said, "Let the little children come to Me, and do not hinder them, for the kingdom of heaven belongs to such as these." (Matt. 19:14 NIV)

If you're a maximizer, you're probably intent on sucking the marrow from every moment and opportunity. You're also quick to beat yourself up for not achieving all you've set out to achieve. I only know this because, on a day when I have, say, eleven things on my to-do list, I'm appalled if I only achieve three of them.

It is possible that what really happened on that unmaximized day were some amazing – slow – deliberate – moments with my kids. And some pausing in the margins of a busy day to listen to a friend. Maybe the better question to ask is, "Am I maximizing each moment, *relationally*?" Relationships don't always fit into tidy calendar slots, but they're the stuff of life. It's our community and connections we should be maximizing most of all.

God, remind me that not everything crucial to life can be ticked off a list. Amen.

Garden self

Now the man and his wife were both naked,
but they felt no shame. (Gen. 2:25 NLT)

What would you have looked like in the Garden of Eden? I don't mean the naked you. I mean, you, *pre-sin*. What's the best, most beautiful version of you – without pride or fear or selfish ambition or jealousy or anger or greed?

If we can get a glimpse of what might have been – and what God might be shaping in us as He restores us over all our earth-side days until that final transformation into our eternal, glorified selves – that might change how we act and react. How we treat others. What we say and how we say it. Decisions and discernment. In weird, difficult, tense, spotlight moments, ask yourself: *What would the Garden of Eden version of me do?*

And when others misunderstand you, reject you, insult you, offend you or disregard you, pretend a little. Treat them like you would in eternity, where you and they will be perfect.

Jesus, remind me that You see the garden me.
You've eradicated my sin:
renewed me and restored me. Amen.

Bedrock

... He set my feet on a rock and gave me
a firm place to stand. (Ps. 40:2 NIV)

As a kid I loved boulder-hopping and rock-clambering. That experience always resonates somewhere in my soul because it reflects our reality as Jesus-lovers. The firmness beneath our feet is the bedrock of Christ. We stand on the Rock of our salvation.

When we remember we are standing on solid rock, we do not need to hang onto other people for balance. We don't have to rely on them to hold us up or support us, because we're entirely comfortable, steady and stable. The rock is beneath our feet all the time, so we are not focused on ourselves or our feelings of security. We're able to enjoy and appreciate wholeheartedly the people in our lives, without setting them up for failure by expecting their love to make us feel safe.

God, show me who I'm leaning on unfairly
or unrealistically. Thank You for putting
terra firma beneath my feet. Amen.

Discern to deliver

Discretion will protect you, and understanding will guard you. (Prov. 2:11 NIV)

Maybe you have someone who notices things. You have the gift of prophecy – or discernment – or insight – or gut feel. You're seldom wrong about the emotional vibes you pick up in a room. You detect people's pain or insecurity or anger – which is when it's good to remember that mercy triumphs over judgment (James 2:13).

If you perceive something negative in your boss, your husband, or your best friend from school, rather pray the positive opposite for him or her. Ask God why He may have highlighted for you another person's challenge or crisis. For sure, it's not for you to judge. It's not necessarily for you to confront that person. It's definitely not for you to share with anyone else.

Rather, ask God to use you to call out the gold in that person. Ask Him to help you counter the negativity with words of wisdom and compassion. No situation is beyond His redemption.

Great Deliverer, nothing's impossible for You!
Lend me discernment so I can see
Your Kingdom come. Amen.

Stuffed

How excellent is Thy lovingkindness,
O God! (Ps. 36:7 KJV)

When you have had a great meal, you do not think about food. Your hunger is satisfied – so you are unaware of it. In the same way, when you are filled up with satisfying life, you don't obsess about you and your life and how things could be, because you are content – *satiated*. You are able to focus on others, pouring out your life in comfort and companionship.

And the unparalleled characteristic of Jesus Christ's abundant life in us is that *it leaves no room for anything else*. When we enjoy the assurance that we're brim-filled with the good life of a good God, there is no more space for fear. No space for pride or arrogance. No space for shame, insecurity, neediness, lack of affection or affirmation or approval, jealousy, greed, comparison, insults.

None of those things can get stuck anywhere in us because we're full up with life. We simply don't have space for them.

God, I couldn't eat another thing!
Thank You for filling me up. Amen.

Crowns laid down

You will be a crown of splendor in the
Lord's hand, a royal diadem in the hand
of your God. (Isa. 62:3 NIV)

I once saw a member of the royal family in our local supermarket. I was struck by how completely down to earth he was.

The people I'm most drawn to are always humble. Unassuming. And secure. Because they're secure – knowing who they are, and Whose they are – they don't need to keep telling you. Imagine a plain-clothes president picnicking with his family in the park. You'd be a little gob-smacked, right?

Knowing our worth – knowing we're really royalty – means we're quite comfortable to lay down our crowns before the throne of the God who bestowed them. We don't constantly need to parade the bling tiaras of our accolades.

Knowing we've already received all those crowns from the only One whose approval matters means we don't need approval from everyone else.

King of kings, I'm so grateful for the crown
You've placed on my head that I'm leaving
it here at Your feet. Amen.

Stories

But they will have to give account to Him
who is ready to judge the living and
the dead. (1 Pet. 4:5 NIV)

In *The Horse and His Boy*, Aslan, the great lion (and allegorical Christ), scratches the girl, Aravis, with his enormous claws. Her friend Shasta asks why. Aslan replies, "Child ... I am telling you your story, not hers. I tell no one any story but his own."

Every breathing human has baggage. Now and then we get a glimpse of the baggage someone else is carrying – a glimpse of what God is doing or apparently not doing in their life. But He wants to draw our eyes to the story *we* are living. We're not responsible or accountable for the stories of others. He doesn't owe us an explanation for the blessing He bestows or the pain He allows in another's journey.

You probably have more than enough sorting to do in your own life, from your own bags. You can confidently leave the contents of another's suitcase full of stories to the One who wrote them.

God, thank You that I only have
to live my own story. Amen.

Carry another's bags

We who are strong ought to bear with the failings of the weak and not to please ourselves. (Rom. 15:1 NIV)

To say that we each live only our own story, *and* that we should carry one another's burdens, is not a contradiction. We don't need to understand fully God's work in another's life; we just need to serve them. It just means seeing a need – and stepping in to do what you can to meet it.

Carry someone's bags by praying for them, or mowing their lawn, or being kind to their difficult kids. Sure, you might be putting yourself at risk by carrying their bags – just as you're at risk in an airport when someone asks you to carry their bags and those bags may or may not contain illicit drugs.

And sure, carrying someone's bags is seldom convenient or comfortable. Carrying the baggage of our sin to the cross wasn't convenient or comfortable for Jesus, either.

Jesus, today, please show me
whose bags I need to carry,
to help carry their load. Amen.

Drama-free queen

So get rid of all evil behavior. Be done with all deceit, hypocrisy, jealousy, and all unkind speech. (1 Pet. 2:1 NLT)

The world loves drama. There's something in all of us that's drawn to a spectacle. And yet, you wouldn't want to be called a drama queen. We all know it's not an attractive quality – to be that woman, always hustling for the scoop and slightly unhinged with hysteria.

The best way to drop the drama baggage is to pick up wisdom. That means, in those situations where you're tempted to give in to the weird stimulation of sensationalism, rather ask yourself: *What's the wise thing to do?*

Considering what I've seen, heard and experienced in the past – considering my present context and the truth about my current circumstances – and considering what I'm hoping to achieve in the future, or the story I hope to tell one day – what is my wisest (and possibly less dramatic) move, right now?

God, I don't need to be in on all the action or the scandal. Give me wisdom to make my next move. Amen.

Important people do

The Lord looks down from heaven on the entire human race; He looks to see if anyone is truly wise, if anyone seeks God. (Ps. 14:2 NLT)

It's a lie that important people get to do important things. *Truly* important people are those *already doing* important things. That's what makes them important. The fact that they're doing things of eternal value – things bigger than themselves – that's what sets them up to leverage their influence.

They're not just elevated by *self*-importance, or *inherited* importance. They're also free from scandal and sensationalism – because they're not focused on themselves and the next rush. They're focused on others, and on somehow improving the world.

Of all the people you know, or know of, who do you consider important? Are they just self-important – or are they *really* important? Are they just celebrities – or have they garnered significance because they're making a significant difference?

God, help me forget about being important.
Show me how to do important things –
for Your Kingdom and glory. Amen.

Success story

Love never fails. (1 Cor. 13:8 NIV)

Real success is a lifelong aspiration towards what Henri Nouwen called downward mobility. Nouwen was once invited to the White House. He declined because he had a disabled friend who needed him.

That's *downward mobility* – and a crazy classification for success. Yet God-defined success is a lowering – not a ladder-climbing. Going to the White House isn't always wrong – so long as our going makes us more like Jesus who was over-qualified to wash feet but did it anyway, with great love. Nothing's beneath us. People who realize that are the kind of humans we all love best.

"Love never fails," writes Paul. *It works every time.* Love never leaves the heart that loves or is loved, the same. It changes us and others. Even if the shop attendant glares at your kind hello, her heart is surely better affected, even if unwittingly, than if *you'd* glared at her. Love is our highest triumph and achievement, guaranteed to outlast every other success.

God, I pray for resounding success as I dive
low to live and love like You. Amen.

Not another step

Moses said, "If Your presence doesn't take the lead here, call this trip off right now." (Ex. 33:15 MSG)

Moses didn't want to take another step into the desert without the assurance that God's presence would lead them – and hem them in from behind (Ps. 139:5).

Daily praying this prayer for God's presence helps divest us of the baggage that weighs down our decision-making around which direction to take. If you're a Jesus-follower then the Holy Spirit is in you, so of course you take His presence with you wherever you go. But what Moses is talking about here is more than God's indwelling presence in the hearts and minds and lives of believers.

It's the dispensation of grace that accompanies us when we're in the center of His will, doing and being what He's called us to do and be, and going where He's called us to go.

Heavenly Father, before I step into today,
align my path with Your strategies
and perfect plans. Amen.

Midlife crisis

He has also set eternity in the human heart ... (Eccles. 3:11 NIV)

Maybe you're wondering if there's more to life than this – or if this is as good as it gets? Because you're sleep-deprived and soul-depleted from kid-raising and you're not even sure you have interests of your own anymore. Your body can't do what it used to do and doesn't look how it used to look.

People say you're just getting comfortable in your own skin but you long for a tighter fit. You're juggling kids and crazy but beneath all the frenetic – monotony seeps insidious. You're living with an acute case of full-blown, terminal life.

And you're coming into fullness. A new, beautiful depth of experience. When you were younger you only saw half the truth – that there's hope, beauty and possibility in this world. Now you're living the privilege of older and now you have a fuller picture of the truth: yes, there's hope, beauty and possibility in this world, but their transient manifestation is just a stunning reflection of the hope, beauty and possibility of an everlasting future.

God, this is more than a midlife crisis.
It's eternity in my heart. Thank You! Amen.

Hard

"Look, I am sending you out as sheep among wolves. So be as shrewd as snakes and harmless as doves." (Matt. 10:16 NLT)

It's possibly occurred to you that Jesus-followers have to carry the heaviest bags of all. Around you are folks who don't value morality or accountability so they're doing whatever they want and loving Jesus can feel boring and exhausting and – *is it worth it*?

You're not the only one living with raw questions and half-baked answers. You're not the only one comparing your real to the highlight reels of Fake-book and reeling from the realization that life really is hard, like God and your parents told you it would be.

Be brave. Jesus never said following Him would result in an easy life. In fact, often when we follow Jesus, life does get harder. But the suffering we endure now is daily racking up in eternity a weight of glory that far outweighs our earthly experiences.

Jesus, I'm finding it hard to live righteous. Help me trust You that a lifetime rooted in joyful obedience results in a rich harvest of freedom from the entanglements of sin. Amen.

Beat defeat

Finally, be strong in the Lord and in His mighty power. (Eph. 6:10 NIV)

To defeat defeatist thinking that says life is hard and getting harder, *find wonder again*. And refuse to lose your sense of awe at who God is and how He splashes splendor across the skies and our hearts.

Keep hunting for beauty. Keep scratching out thank-You-God moments in your journal or your Instagram stories, even if people think you're weird. Keep teaching your kids and your colleagues to notice and revel and reach for the mystery. All this present glory tugs at our sleeves – points eagerly to the unfading glory to come. Don't let the sadness wash over you for what might have been. The best is yet to be.

And *get dirty*. Dig deep into the life soil of your kids and your community. Don't be afraid to get your hands muddy for Kingdom causes bigger than you. Live unveiled, unfettered, unhurried. Sow generously all God has sown in you.

Jesus, I praise You that wonder is weightless, and service sets us free. Help me travel light with those truths in mind. Amen.

Baggage to beauty

He does great things too marvelous to understand.
He performs countless miracles. (Job 5:9 NLT)

In the midst of difficulty, determine not to grow weary of doing good. In due time you'll reap. In due time, you may even have more time. And new direction and opportunity. Don't give up now.

Paul – persecuted – wrote, "We now have this light shining in our hearts, but we ourselves are like fragile clay jars containing this great treasure. This makes it clear that our great power is from God, not from ourselves. We are pressed on every side by troubles, but we are not crushed. We are perplexed, but not driven to despair" (2 Cor. 4:7-9 NLT).

You are not the only one facing what you face. But there is only One who can turn your doubt and disappointment into deeper devotion, your drudgery into dreams, your despair into post-traumatic growth. He's your courage to face what isn't fair. He's the catalyst for lasting change. He is your hope.

God, I know You can turn baggage into beauty.
Take the mess of my burst-open bags
and make a miracle of me. Amen.

Head spread

... we take captive every thought to make it obedient to Christ. (2 Cor. 10:5 NIV)

If you've spent even five minutes in the last 24 hours wondering (or mildly obsessing over) what someone thought about what you said, did or texted – this is for you.

Paul says we shouldn't let trash talk spew from our mouths. We should only say what's helpful, encouraging and strengthening (Eph. 4:29). But what comes out of our mouths starts in our heads, which is why Paul also says we should make every thought a happy prisoner of Jesus.

So I'm asking myself, *What rumors am I spreading in my head*? I dare not believe everything I think. You can control the stories you tell yourself. Tell yourself the true stories God tells about you. Like, He delights in you, calms your fears, and sings over your life (Zeph. 3:17), and you can hide in the shadow of His wings, knowing He'll fulfill His purposes for you (Ps. 57:1).

Lord, shine a truth laser on the lies that have darkened my thinking. Amen.

Rumor to revolution

Do not let any unwholesome talk come out of your mouths, but only what is helpful for building others up according to their needs, that it may benefit those who listen. (Eph. 4:29 NIV)

Sometimes rumors are all in the mind; sometimes they're real. People's abrupt responses or lack of interest are, mostly, because they're swathed in their own stress and they *just can't even*. There's not a lot of emotional capacity going around these days, for people to stop and show you they care.

But revolutions start with crazies like us who think it is possible to break the cycle of disinterest and apathy. Make right with people you've wronged. Be real, trust God to protect your reputation, and smile.

It'll hurt at first – like hiking with blisters. You put your boots on and think you'll never move again. You hobble for a mile or two. Then you walk those blisters in. You absorb the pain and start noticing beauty. You realize the rumors aren't running wild anymore. And you're running free.

God, work Your wonders in
rumor-ridden relationships. Amen.

Kid baggage

I remember your genuine faith, for you share the faith that first filled your grandmother Lois and your mother, Eunice. And I know that same faith continues strong in you. (2 Tim. 1:5 NLT)

Maybe, like Timothy, you grew up in a healthy home: well-balanced and well-loved. Possibly, you grew up spoiled and entitled. Or, you grew up ignored, abandoned, disregarded or abused.

We all carry childhood bags we need to open up and sort out. Some of our baggage must be burned. Some items should be washed, ironed, folded and put away. Some needs to be lovingly held up to our cheeks so we can smell the good memories and appreciate the legacy.

Be brave. Unzip your childhood. God was there in every moment. Whether you believed in Him or not – acknowledged Him or not – He never took His eyes off you. He shares in the happiness, and He's willing to carry the heaviness.

Father, thank You that nothing in my past slipped through the safety net of Your sovereignty, unbidden. My childhood is part of the story You're writing with my life. Amen.

Optimism for the win

... while we look forward with hope to that wonderful day when the glory of our great God and Savior, Jesus Christ, will be revealed. (Tit. 2:13 NLT)

I used to believe that the future would always be better than the past. Nowadays, I know the future *isn't always* better than the past – if we think *better* means *happier* or in sync with what *we* think is best for us.

A future rendered to the Heavenly Father – lived in the slipstream of His power, wisdom and love – is bigger, richer, deeper, and fantastically colored-in outside-the-lines. The future reroutes us from our naive, two-dimensional ideals, and in that, God blesses us to bless the world.

Don't give up. Today is a slice of the future that once gnawed at your gut. Now it's here, served with a side of supersize grace. Each single-minded one-foot-in-front-of-the-other will get you to the next breathtaking view – and eventually, eternity. Relax into the rhythm of the road and know that ours is a future that's free and everlasting.

Jesus, I can't wait to find You
in my future! Amen.

Beautiful boundaries

The boundary lines have fallen for me in pleasant places; surely I have a delightful inheritance. (Ps. 16:6 NIV)

A friend had to share her study with her two kids. They were all over her things – using up her space and her stationery and her patience. So she divided the workspace into three with colored ribbons. She got them their own stationery and turned it all into a celebration.

She was astounded at how those few boundaries brought *life*. They taught her kids how to fill their space and how to fill it well, beautifully and appropriately. Once they understood what was theirs to own, they did a great job, managing their allotment.

We tend to see boundaries as negative restrictions: *this far and no further*! We feel guilty about setting up boundaries in our lives. But actually, boundaries give birth to beautiful things like order, respect, responsibility and breathe-easy love.

God, show me where the lines in my relationships or responsibilities have been unhealthily blurred. Teach me how to lay down beautiful boundaries that result in greater love and life. Amen.

Live in the light

And we all, who with unveiled faces contemplate the Lord's glory, are being transformed into His image with ever-increasing glory. (2 Cor. 3:18 NIV)

You absolutely do have the right to privacy. Some things are sacred and special and need only be shared with a trusted few, or a trusted one, or God alone.

Yet as believers we have a mandate to live in the light – with "unveiled faces". The truth is, no one walks away from Jesus because of Jesus. They walk away from Jesus because of people who say they follow Jesus, but who aren't taking seriously the responsibility of living pure lives. So maybe it shouldn't worry us that Google knows everything about us, because we should have nothing to hide.

In fact, the notion of large corporations violating our privacy by trawling through our Facebook accounts or messaging platforms might even excite us, because maybe in the words and photos and memes and likes, they'll come across something of Jesus.

God, I want to live in the light, so that anyone looking at my life will see You, lit. Amen.

Evening offering

"Sacrifice one lamb in the morning and the other in the evening." (Num. 28:4 NLT)

A mentor of mine encouraged me to give the Father an evening offering. The idea comes from the Hebrew practice of morning and evening sacrifice. Before drifting off to sleep – when my brain is sifting through the day and slowing down – I try to remember to ask, "Lord, what pleased You today?" And then, "Lord, what didn't please You today?"

You will be amazed how the day's moments will surface almost immediately: the God-honoring moments of love or difficult obedience – those things that pleased Him. And then those things that didn't – the harsh word, the impatience or greed.

Leaving at the King's feet the things that delighted Him helps you not to get proud. It reminds you that you did them for Him anyway, not for you. And leaving at His feet those things that didn't delight Him helps you repent quickly – running into the reprieve of His grace and forgiveness.

Yahweh, thank You that I'm not defined by today's success or failure, and that tomorrow I'll wake up to new mercies. Amen.

Just say no

"Stop at the crossroads and look around ... Travel its path, and you will find rest for your souls. But you reply, 'No, that's not the road we want!'" (Jer. 6:16 NLT)

We face a plethora of overwhelming options, and to live in-the-light lives, we need to pray for some clarity on what we should and shouldn't be choosing. Let's be intentional about seeking wisdom and simplicity, because sure, we can do anything, but we can't do everything, and we certainly can't do it all, have it all, and be it all, today.

It may be easier for you to manage your yeses well, when you can get it right to disinvest from what people might think of your no. Sometimes it's important to consider the impact of a decision on your reputation, and sometimes you need to take ownership of your capacity and your unique context, and just say no.

God, I want to say yes to You today. Give me wisdom and courage, kindness and courtesy, so I can say no if I need to, in a God-glorifying, people-honoring way. Amen.

Get over it

Obviously, I'm not trying to win the approval of people, but of God. (Gal. 1:10 NLT)

Most of us like to think of ourselves as independent, knowing our own minds and not needing validation from others. And yet, if we are properly honest, we cringe when things we say come out wrong and we worry about how our decisions might be received. The humbling thing is that worrying about what others think – wondering if we measure up to their expectations – *that's just pride*.

Ordinary, everyday life is a bit like public speaking. A lot can go wrong on the day. You don't know for sure who your audience will be and how your message will be heard. Perhaps the best thing we can do, to live with confidence and courage, is get over ourselves and aim all our sayings and doings at the audience of One: the only audience that really matters. Let's focus first on connecting with Him – then on communicating with others.

Jesus, I want to live to please You.
If I get to please people as well,
that's just a bonus. Amen.

Hope declared

And this hope will not lead to disappointment. For we know how dearly God loves us, because He has given us the Holy Spirit to fill our hearts with His love. (Rom. 5:5 NLT)

If you tend towards optimism, it's easy to put your hope in a bunch of other things. And if you tend towards pessimism, you're probably more likely to lose hope altogether. Both options lead to disappointment.

But Paul tells us there's a hope that *does not disappoint*, and His name is Jesus. So, if we've been disappointed – and of course we have been, and of course we will be again – our hope was in the wrong thing. It's ok to be disappointed. It's inevitable. But let's decide today to keep on declaring the truth that there's still, always, the hope that does not disappoint.

Jesus, it's such a relief that no matter what happens in this world, I will always have hope, because I will always have You. Amen.

Keep it real

"Seek the Kingdom of God above
all else, and He will give you everything
you need." (Luke 12:31 NLT)

Social media is a stunning invention. It connects people and gives us a means of instantaneously sharing news, sharing love, and sharing Jesus. But Facebook and other platforms have seen to it that we're frothing to let the world know what we're doing, and how beautifully or perfectly we're doing it.

Slide your screen off a little more often. Work at doing real life as wonderfully well as possible. What is God saying to you, today? What's the work He has cut out for you? Do it. Take seriously your personal holiness – becoming more and more like Jesus.

Seek first the Kingdom. The rest will take care of itself. And when you lift your head there will be fruit hanging low and ripe from your beautiful branches. Better than pixels – it'll be ready for actual people, to actually pick.

God, let's keep it real. Help me to be authentic:
not pretending perfection, but rather just living,
loving and doing life for You. Amen.

Declaring others

I have not stopped thanking God for you.
I pray for you constantly. (Eph. 1:16 NLT)

The most effective way out of the heaviness and darkness of self is to celebrate someone else. I heard it said once of an eminent leader: "He makes other people the hero, which is what all great communicators do." And you're communicating all day, every day.

Through loud opinions or disinterested silences – you're sending a message to the world around you. Your every action and attitude says something about your values, priorities and state of being.

Could you step out into the spotlight on the stage of today and sing someone's praises? Take the focus off yourself. Make another human the hero. Be an excellent communicator by declaring the loveliness of someone else.

Almighty God, let the message of my life be loud and clear. I want to be all about honoring others and glorifying You. Amen.

Word worship

I am not ashamed of this Good News
about Christ. It is the power of God at work,
saving everyone who believes – the Jew first
and also the Gentile. (Rom. 1:16 NLT)

My youngest son once asked me, of someone who had come to visit, "Is he a Christian?" I said, "Um, I think he is." Surprised, my son replied, "Oh. But he never really talks about God?"

No one had overtly explained it, but he'd somehow absorbed the truth that we talk about what we worship. Without faking it or contriving our piety, we can naturally give it away – who or what we worship – with our words.

Solomon writes, "Do not be quick with your mouth, do not be hasty in your heart to utter anything before God. God is in heaven and you are on earth, so let your words be few" (Eccles. 5:2 NIV). While we should unquestionably choose our words well, when we do use them, they should reflect a world view in which God is on the throne.

Jesus, teach me how to season my
conversations with the flavor of You. Amen.

Set apart

You made me; You created me. Now give me the sense to follow Your commands. (Ps. 119:73 NLT)

You are unique. You're never-before, never-again. God says, "I knew you before I formed you in your mother's womb. Before you were born I set you apart" (Jer. 1:5 NLT). He says that He made all the inside and the outside bits of you (Ps. 139:13), that every hair on your head is numbered (Matt. 10:30) and that He has plans for you (Jer. 29:11). That should completely blow our minds.

It's not that God *needs* us. He's the all-sufficient sustainer of the universe. It's just astounding and humbling and so very exciting that He sees fit to make us, love us and use us as part of His coming Kingdom on this planet. God has created a position for you in His organization. Just like everyone else, you've been set apart for a marvelous, God-designed purpose.

God, I can't believe You'd want to use me uniquely to spread Your name and Your fame. Thank You for delighting in making me different. Amen.

Not about you

O Lord, our Lord, Your majestic name fills the earth! Your glory is higher than the heavens. When I look at the night sky and see the work of Your fingers – the moon and the stars You set in place – what are mere mortals that You should think about them? (Ps. 8:1, 3-4 NLT)

Your uniqueness isn't about you. You get to do your very own life's work and live out your very own shimmering destiny. But whether you're hilarious, smart, sensitive or gregarious: all of that loveliness points to your King.

The small white miracle that is each inimitable snowflake doesn't point to the greatness of the snowflake. It points to the greatness of the One who made it. Your startling, powerful uniqueness points to the genius of the One who encoded your DNA.

Your unique gifts are yours, but not for you. They're to be used for others, and for the glory of God.

God, thank You that we're all distinct from one another.
I want to live that individuality in such a way
that it increases the influence of
Your Kingdom on earth. Amen.

Declaring dependence

O LORD, I give my life to You. (Ps. 25:1 NLT)

The Bible does not actually have much to say about independence. It does talk about how in Christ we're independent from sin. It does talk about working independently with our own hands for our own money.

But mostly, the Bible talks about dependence, and dependability. Throughout the God-story, we read about our desperate *dependence* on a Savior, and how His character forged in us makes us *dependable*.

The Word pours stories of community, communion and companionship. Stories about how we're created to need each other's strength and trustworthiness. Stories about how the world will wonder Who we follow. They'll watch us loving each other. And they'll know (John 13:35). Independence is important. It is right-sized self-assurance that lends us the stability to be dependable. But we dare not let it mutate into arrogance or self-sufficiency, thinking we're invincible, or above needing the help or accountability of others. How cool, rather, to be known for our courageous dependability on our Redeemer.

Lord God, make me dependable,
and wholly dependent on You. Amen.

Little pencil

We are the clay, and You are the potter. (Isa. 64:8 NLT)

Mother Teresa wrote, "I'm a little pencil in the hand of a writing God, who is sending a love letter to the world ... He does the writing. He does everything and sometimes it is really hard because it is a broken pencil and He has to sharpen it a little more."

She was all about being the little pencil. She was a *broken* pencil and she knew ultimately there'd be no trace left of her in this world. Only the marks of *Him*. And she was totally ok with that.

You and I absolutely have to get out of our *own* way so God can work out – not *our* purposes – but *His* purposes, through us. When we surrender to the only God who can make something meaningful of our lives – when we stop investing so heavily in our ambitions and agendas – it's remarkably liberating.

Disentangled from self-interest, we're fantastically free to go where He sends, and do as He does.

God, take what lead is left in this
little life. Do all the writing. Amen.

Love-defiant

Whoever does not love does not know God,
because God is love. (1 John 4:8 NIV)

We might meet some strange people as we go through life. People who make us wonder what happened to them to make them like they are.

God wastes nothing – least of all our every human interaction. Love never fails (1 Cor. 13:8), so even though we might walk away from love-defiant people feeling ineffective, the Father sees the heart. He sees our hearts, genuinely loving and respecting the love-defiant. But He sees the love-defiant person's heart too. And if enough people heap love on the love-defiant – the genuine, relentless affection of the Father who runs to us, to rescue us – it might all add up to some kind of wonderful tipping point.

We tend to underestimate the power of the Father's presence – forgetting we take it with us wherever we go. And so wherever we go maybe we have got to ask ourselves, What does love look like, in this place, at this time?

Lord, let it be that whoever I interact with today,
I leave them somehow different,
by choosing to love. Amen.

Catch the light

Those who look to Him for help will be radiant with joy; no shadow of shame will darken their faces. (Ps. 34:5 NLT)

Diamonds are multi-faceted. That's what makes them sparkle and shine as they catch the light. Bits of them have been cut away, polished, and angled into different surfaces.

Your life is multi-faceted too. You may be a wife, mom, friend, sister, daughter, employer ... And you're thinking, *All those facets of my life don't make me sparkly; they make me exhausted.* But don't lose heart or stop dreaming.

God is shaping you. Polishing you. Cutting away bits of you to make something beautiful as you trust Him to position you in those different arenas, for His glory.

God calls us to shine in all facets of our lives – and maybe He's convicting you in one particular area? And what has become dull and unpolished? Could you take one beautiful step towards polishing what needs a new shine by asking one trusted friend to pray for you – for that facet of your life?

God, polish every facet of me,
until I shine. Amen.

Hard as diamonds

So, my dear brothers and sisters, be strong and immovable. Always work enthusiastically for the Lord, for you know that nothing you do for the Lord is ever useless. (1 Cor. 15:58 NLT)

The word *diamond* is from the Latin *adamans* from which we get adamant.

Jeremy Courtney tells the story of how he and his family moved to Iraq after 9/11, and then to Syria, just to be Jesus to a devastated people. Jeremy founded the Pre-emptive Love Coalition. Their mission is that, wherever there's violence and war, they're the first people there and the last to leave.

He talks about seeing people, instead of seeing problems – about moving into a neighborhood and loving the way Jesus loved. In doing so, he and his wife and his young children have been shot at by snipers and there isn't a day when he isn't afraid. But, he says, "You move fear to the passenger seat. You keep driving. And you love anyway."

That's unshakeable, immovable, inflexible, unwavering, uncompromising, resolute, resolved, determined, steadfast, firm *diamond* faith.

O God, give me rock hard, glittering,
world-changing faith! Amen.

Darkness, heat and pressure

We are pressed on every side by troubles, but we are not crushed. We are perplexed, but not driven to despair. (2 Cor. 4:8 NLT)

To make a diamond, you need extreme pressure, incredibly hot temperatures, in the dark, for a long time.

Have you experienced – at some point in your life, or now – intense heat and pressure and stress in your life? Do you feel like God's left you in the dark, and like it's gone on for far, far too long? Paul writes, "We are pressed on every side by troubles, but we are not crushed." When you are pressed on every side, it is possible that God is forming something beautiful and unbreakable – uncrushable – in you.

Breathe deep even as the pressure mounts. He will not let you be crushed.

God, I feel like this thing is squeezing the life out of me. Help me believe that You won't let it finish me, and You won't leave me in the darkness, heat or pressure forever. Amen.

A girl's best friend

For you have been given not only the privilege of trusting in Christ but also the privilege of suffering for Him. (Phil. 1:29 NLT)

I don't say this flippantly, but it's possible we need to see darkness, heat and pressure as a gift. A friend. We can befriend suffering because it's part of our royal inheritance as daughters of the King who really suffered, for us.

Job is a great example of someone who lived a fantastic life and suffered unbelievably. He went through intense heat, darkness and pressure, for a good long while. The rocks around his life were pressing him on every side. He didn't feel sparkly and strong. He felt shocked, sad and angry.

But in the end – before God restored everything (Job 42:12) and while he was still a hot mess – Job recognized that his hope should be in God, not in the geological conditions of his life. So in the end, the heat, pressure and darkness didn't shake his identity or his relationship with God.

Father, help me befriend suffering because of what it produces in me. Amen.

Hurry up and wait

Wait patiently for the LORD. Be brave and courageous. Yes, wait patiently for the LORD. (Ps. 27:14 NLT)

It seems no matter what our life's circumstances, God makes us wait. His chief concerns are His glory, His Kingdom, and transforming us into His likeness. Waiting renders in us a kind of transformation that nothing else does.

So we wait for the Heavenly Father. We wait for others. We wait for dreams to come true and desires to be fulfilled. We wait for clarity and resolution, help and healing. We wait for eternity.

Now and then God surprises us with a swift orchestration of events and we go, "Whoa! That was fast! God's really moving!" But mostly, He works unhurriedly – because we're quick to forget and slow to trust. Or because He's fashioning unseen, background plans, or crafting in us the beauty of patient surrender.

God, show me if I should wait passively – letting go entirely and waiting for You to work – or actively – by working while I wait. Amen.

Obscurity or exhibition

So whether you eat or drink, or whatever you do, do it all for the glory of God. (1 Cor. 10:31 NLT)

The hardest thing about waiting can be not knowing what God is up to. We're not sure if or when we'll see the results or rewards of our efforts, and if those efforts even matter.

Like, perhaps you have a platform of international influence. Or perhaps you're scanning barcodes at a checkout. In the eyes of the King who has welcomed you into His royal household as a child and heir – both of those activities are of absolute and equal significance. You don't know what hangs in the balance of either of those pursuits.

Whether the Father has you waiting for the next big thing, or in the midst of a big thing, just as much is at stake. Live those moments as if every small or big thing is a Kingdom thing.

Lord, whether I'm winning, or waiting in the wings, I'm going to do it for You. Amen.

Mandatory waiting

Then Jesus said, "Let's go off by ourselves to a quiet place and rest awhile." He said this because there were so many people coming and going that Jesus and His apostles didn't even have time to eat. (Mark 6:31 NLT)

Sometimes waiting is forced upon us. We don't get a say about when we wait, or for how long. And sometimes we need to be intentional about building into our lives times to rest, and reset, and allow our souls to catch up with our bodies.

Our culture is bent on sweeping us into all things fast and frenetic. But we don't need to believe the lie that if every waking moment isn't filled with something measurable or profitable, we're being idle.

The Kingdom way of living is counter-culture. Instead of being maniacally industrious at the expense of health and reason, we can exhibit calm, and rest, and unforced rhythms of grace (Matt. 11:28-30).

Jesus, take over my calendars and agendas.
Give me ways and wisdom to block out chunks of time – waiting on You, waiting on others. Amen.

Catch your breath

Be still before the LORD and wait
patiently for Him. (Ps. 37:7 NIV)

It's really ok to give yourself a break once in a while. You can't change the bed sheets and people's minds and the world, all in one day. It's ok not to multi-task (which is really nothing more than task-switching – which lowers productivity). Rather, do each slow steady thing as if it's the only thing, and do it excellently.

There's a lot of noise out there, and in our heads. Mahatma Gandhi said, "Speak only if it improves upon the silence." Breathe more deeply, more often. And pause before you re-enter the fray, so the truth can steady you: there's enough time today to do God's will.

Life is not an emergency and God is not in a rush. The things you're trying frantically to achieve may not ultimately matter. Waiting around for just a little bit, to catch your breath, is just fine.

God, don't let me get ahead of myself –
sacrificing my strength and emotional wellbeing
on the altar of productivity. I'll worship
You and walk at Your pace. Amen.

Unwasted time

We know that God causes everything to work together for the good of those who love God and are called according to His purpose for them. (Rom. 8:28 NLT)

When you find yourself in the in-between – a season of waiting, deliberating, or being subject to debilitating unknowns – it's still possible to live joyfully and intentionally, making sure that this time isn't pointless. For a start, don't begin a day until it's surrendered to God in prayer. Plan something helpful and meaningful, every day, despite the tedium of the wait you're enduring, and despite the uncertainty you face.

By consistently setting small goals you can confidently ensure that you never have a "zero day" – a wasted, utterly unsuccessful chunk of life spent and forever behind you. Faith, a positive attitude and maximum effort go a long way to ensuring that you don't become lethargic while waiting. Waiting needn't equal stagnation. It could be a joy-infused time of rest, and preparation.

God, thank You that You're the God who wastes nothing. Redeem this unused time. Turn it into something unusually useful – for Your glory. Amen.

Waiting for the call

The world and all its people belong to Him. (Ps. 24:1 NLT)

Even if your today looks the same as yesterday and tomorrow promises more of the same, God cares for you in your humdrum circumstances as much as He cares for anyone else in any other small spot of this planet.

Holly Gerth writes, "God doesn't value a far-off there more than an ordinary and near here. And every *there* for us is someone else's *here*." Other people's callings can seem exotic, yet we're *all* missionaries because we're all on foreign consignment, waiting for the call home to heaven.

Holly goes on to say, "We do not have to go anywhere but to Him in order for us to be useful in His Kingdom. For those called to step on a plane or a train or boat, go with the blessing of God. For those called to stay in a kitchen or a conference room, stay with the blessing of God."

God, I'm amazed and excited that
no matter where You have me standing,
I stand on holy ground. Amen.

Wait for yes

Wait for the LORD and keep His way ... (Ps. 37:34 ESV)

Some years back, after too many unnecessary yeses, I took stock of what I should and shouldn't agree to, for the sake of my family and my sanity. I decided to assume the response to every request was no, unless God gave me a clear directive that it was yes.

It didn't feel selfish, because God also made it clear that with every yes I should be laying myself down for another – the way He would.

If you're human, you've probably wrestled with saying no. But hopefully God is pointing out your blind spots and the places you're stuck, and you're learning the importance of boundaries and shaking off the impulse to say yes to every invitation or opportunity.

Living in the *no*-zone isn't an unwillingness to serve. Rather, it's a way to wait on God for the very best yes, and a way to make all the yeses more intentional acts of worship.

God, help me create margin to think
and better steward my gifts, by waiting
wisely for the right yes. Amen.

Placed not abandoned

Do not be afraid or terrified ... for the Lord your God goes with you; He will never leave you nor forsake you. (Deut. 31:6 NIV)

Times of waiting can feel horribly like abandonment. And it's easy, in times when what you long for is elusive or entirely absent, to assume that the Father has forgotten you. That He has stopped loving you and stopped being in control of your life.

Let this truth be the wind in your sails: God will never forsake you or move on without you. He will never show up late or overlook a promise. Instead, this hard time of waiting, it's His *placement* of you in the perfect incubator of His plans. He's never not transforming you into the image of His Son.

Jesus spent thirty years in preparation for three years of preaching. Most of our lives are spent preparing, and that's ok. In fact, it's so very good. You're being placed, not abandoned.

God, thank You that You position me – right here where I am – in the waiting. Amen.

In utero

You watched me as I was being formed in utter seclusion, as I was woven together in the dark of the womb. (Ps. 139:15 NLT)

A friend told me she was going to ask her doctor to induce labor, because she was tired of waiting. Pregnancy can feel super long. But I thought, *We're even rushing our children from the womb!* We rush their entrance into a rushed world!

People prefer us to be busy and stressed and run off our feet and worried and weary because that's how they feel. Our world's workforce doesn't generally promote the slow stock-taking of inner reflection. Where God is asking us to linger, the world says hurry. We're a society of instant gratification and we hate to wait.

Wherever, right now, you're experiencing the hindrance or aggravation of waiting, remember that if our children didn't get nine months of dark, quiet womb-transit, they wouldn't survive. Pray, pray, pray into your future hope. Then simply wait on God as He makes you wait.

God, give me patience to let stillness and seclusion do their work. Amen.

Dynamic parenting

She carefully watches everything in her household and suffers nothing from laziness. Her children stand and bless her ... (Prov. 31:27-28 NLT)

Raising kids can feel like one long season of limbo. Of course we see changes in our children as they grow – too fast – and grow into the people the Heavenly Father has created them to be. It's more like a slow dawning – moments of realization that oh-my-word there's actually been a bit of progress.

But as the minutes, months and years tick by until our kids' incubation in our homes comes to an end, there are ways to wait dynamically – ways to invest in their future.

Write out crafted prayers for your kids. Journal the advice you'd love to leave them. Read to them at any and every opportunity and for as long as they'll listen. Ask questions every day.

Then, when the wait is over and they embark on their own big wide world adventures, the wait will have been so worth it, because they'll be set up for success.

God, help me take full advantage of
the time I have with my kids. Amen.

Stalling

Jesus responded, "Didn't I tell you that you would see God's glory if you believe?" (John 11:40 NLT)

Today you might be asking, *Why doesn't God do something about this situation*? I don't have the answer. But I do know He can do something about it. And I know sometimes He waits before He acts. And I know that – meanwhile – in the waiting – you can trust Him.

We place our hope in what we depend on. Keep depending on God. If it seems to you He's stalling? As if He isn't coming through for you quickly enough? Don't start depending on someone else or something else to fulfill your hopes. His ways are perfect, and all His ways are just (Ps. 18:30).

If God seems to be inattentive, uncooperative or late: know that somehow, somewhere, in some way, you will definitely see His glory.

God, help me to be patient and
to trust that You'll come through at
the perfect time. Amen.

Fenced off

You must keep My Sabbath days of rest ... (Lev. 26:2 NLT)

Once a year, a marathon that winds through our city includes our street. Thousands of runners come past our house. We stand on the driveway in our pajamas and watch.

It's a picture of the Sabbath. We're ring-fenced from the rush and running of life barreling on oblivious. It makes me think, *We don't have to be fast or busy today. The world can be fast and busy for one day a week, without us.*

To institute a weekly Sabbath, make some rules. Fence off one day a week. It can be any day. Set a couple of specific boundaries, but don't make it complicated or unrealistic. Like, you might simply decide not to open your laptop, or not to go onto social media on your phone.

When we decide to Sabbath intentionally, the world really does still spin on its axis, even without us swinging in to add to the momentum.

God, help me trust You enough to accept
that it's really ok to do as You say,
and take a day off. Amen.

Break some rules

My heart leaps for joy, and with my song I praise Him. (Ps. 28:7 NIV)

For about a year, we drew ridiculous pictures on the dining room table on Sunday nights. We started doing this the second Sunday of the year, quite by accident. I subsequently bought a dozen rolls of brown paper, and it became something of a Sabbath tradition.

As a rule, one doesn't draw on the dining room table. But this is one of the ways we try to break out, on the Sabbath, of what's done or not done, as a rule. As a rule, no one has three helpings of ice-cream. As a rule, no one has time to go bike riding or bush walking or lawn cricketing on a Sunday.

So we try – just once a week – to get out and do those double-chocolate-caramel-swirl, under-the-sky things, because a twenty percent effort to rest and refuel can make an eighty percent difference to our energy and enthusiasm in the week ahead.

God, show me where I'm rule-bound, and how I can rest. Amen.

Set reminders

Because the Sovereign Lord helps me, I will not be disgraced. Therefore, I have set my face like a stone, determined to do His will. (Isa. 50:7 NLT)

Rest requires a hardcore commitment. You've got to set your face like stone.

Four times a year, my family and I do two or three days of deep rest. It gives us space to go, *Are we all ok? Where have we come from? Where are we going?* Let's catch our breath before we carry on. Every ninety days is also a good time to back up your files, clean up your clouds, use up everything in the freezer and start again. It's astoundingly – surprisingly – restful.

Those rhythms might not work for you, your family or your circle of friends, but for sure, if you don't actively plan some means of rest, somewhere in your schedule, you won't be running your life; your life will be running you.

God, rest is rebellious in this non-stop world – an act of resistance to trends. Help me to be brave and intentional, and make sure it happens. Amen.

In the middle

May the God of endurance and encouragement grant you to live in such harmony with one another .... (Rom. 15:5 ESV)

Life happens in three stages: beginning, middle and end. While God is definitely in all three stages, the middle bit is the longest and the hardest.

Becky Beresford writes, "Our middles are just as important as our beginnings and ends. Sometimes we wish we could bypass the middle and fast-forward to the final chapter where our prayers are answered and our desires fulfilled. But we have such a kind God, and He doesn't waste a single second in our life. He doesn't push the pause button when we feel like life stops moving. He is always working for the good of those who love Him."

I don't know what you're in the middle of, but you're not alone. Everyone you know or meet is in the middle of something. When I remember that, I feel less sorry for myself, and more compassionate towards the people God scripts into my day.

O God, meet me in the middle!
Help me to make it count. Amen.

Stress to stillness

When I refused to confess my sin, my body wasted away, and I groaned all day long. (Ps. 32:3 NLT)

I got shingles over Easter some years ago. Elisabeth Elliot said that we're not laid aside by illness but called aside for stillness. I, however, didn't get the first stillness memo so the shingles reared its painful head for round two.

A stress-related illness was humbling evidence that I hadn't trusted God with the tension in my life. The forced stillness gave me space to reconsider how I managed my time and responsibilities. It reminded me that I had only myself to blame for any stress that had lodged in my mind and infiltrated my body.

Cognitive neuroscientist Dr. Caroline Leaf maintains that the effects of negative thoughts look structurally different, in the brain, from those of positive thoughts. We are what we think, and we are how we talk, and if we want to learn to be still, and stress-free, we need to hold tight to the reins of our runaway thoughts.

God, strengthen my mind to think upon –
and rest in – Your magnificence. Amen.

Balance

Therefore, if anyone is in Christ, the new creation has come. (2 Cor. 5:17 NIV)

As we seek to wait well – to find rest in the middle of life – we need to balance the earthly and the eternal. The limitless God who spoke out light and split the sea lives in limited me, and you. His infinite creativity, infinite love, dwells in our finite hearts and minds. It is what it is, and what it is, is a mystery.

Alli Worthington writes: "When God created us, He created us with a limitless capacity to love others and ... stretch our talents to be used for His glory. He also created us with a body that needs rest, and He placed us in a universe that has a limited number of hours in each day. When we operate under the belief that we can do it all, we're forgetting how God wants us to rely on Him. We're adding so much extra 'noise' to our lives that we can't hear His voice speaking our true calling."

God, do the limitless
in limited me. Amen.

Faith in healing

For we live by faith, not by sight. (2 Cor. 5:7 NIV)

When it comes to healing, we're called to live by faith, as we are in every arena of life. It takes faith to trust that the Father can / does / will heal. It takes faith to trust that if / when / because He doesn't heal, He's still infinitely kind, wise and powerful.

God heals to bolster our faith. He heals even when no one is looking, and sometimes – most times? – He lets brokenness run its course.

I have no idea why. But I do know He's faithful, and perfect in powerful love. It's also comforting to remember that healing gives us a glimpse of God's Kingdom, which is Now and Not Yet. We're in a glorious dispensation of grace and Holy Spirit power – but we ain't seen nothin' yet. If you don't see healing in this life, you'll certainly see it in the next.

God, thank You that healing is a tangible manifestation of what You do on the inside of me – total renewal – and an electrifying reminder of the eternal realities that await. Amen.

No explanation

Jesus asked him, "Would you like to get well?" (John 5:6 NLT)

As you pray and wait for healing or resolution, remember that God invented decision-making and He doesn't owe us an explanation for His perfect decisions.

At the pool of Bethesda there were "crowds of sick people" (John 5:3). Yet Jesus went up to just one man amidst swarms of the sick and the dying – and He healed him. Jesus didn't explain why He picked that one man.

God has been deciding things since forever. He chose Abraham's family – not some other family – to bless the whole world. He chose Moses – not some other guy – to lead His people out of Egypt.

All this has never bothered me because it's never been personal. Yet my Heavenly Father is intensely, intimately personal to me. His power that split the sea and raised the dead is alive in me. However He chooses to reveal Himself through me, to the world? Well, I'm ok with that.

God, You know it all and see it all.
I'm trusting the decisions to You. Amen.

Closure opens

He did not retaliate when He was insulted,
nor threaten revenge when He suffered.
He left His case in the hands of God,
who always judges fairly. (1 Pet. 2:23 NLT)

A friend shared with us that she had been sexually abused as a kid. She realized that there might never be justice in this life for what had been done to her. She needed a brave someone to say what she already feared: that there might never be earthly revenge or restitution. But it brought her closure – knowing there may never be closure. She let it go so she could leave her case in the hands of God.

I pray you'd *open* your heart, stop looking for closure, and start looking for openness. Because to travel light we've got to keep our hearts and lives, our front doors and fridges, *open* to people who deserve our generosity and people who will almost certainly take advantage of it.

God of justice and perfect closure: help me
be ok with the possibility that closure may
only come when You open up for me the
great wide open of eternity. Amen.

Horizon

"I am the Alpha and the Omega – the beginning and the end," says the Lord God. (Rev. 1:8 NLT)

When my husband and I did our first scuba dive, the sea was rough, we were nervous, and the boat lurched, dipped and billowed petrol fumes all over our queasiness. Our dive master told us, "Keep your eyes on the horizon and you won't get sick."

When we're navigating storms, we mustn't look down into the boat where waves crash and fears ask, *Why this storm, God?* We'll seldom find answers in the boat. Mostly, because the story of our suffering is a few sentences in an intricate, sweeping, deeply meaningful and totally un-random plot, the suffering seems pretty random, inefficient and ineffectual.

To make sense of suffering, we've got to look up, and we've got to look far – to the horizon of history – where God will roll up all our stories on that final shore. He will refresh, restore and renew all things – and it will be glorious.

God, thank You that the end
is just the beginning. Amen.

Unstuck by grace

You then, my child, be strengthened by the grace that is in Christ Jesus ... (2 Tim. 2:1 ESV)

It is comforting that grace sticks and secures you. Except, stuck may be exactly what you don't want to be. You don't want to be stuck in your circumstances, not getting the mobility, the ministry or the momentum you crave.

It is refreshing to recall that the Father's grace is changing grace. When grace arrests your heart, it begins to change you. Grace is more than pardon. It's power. Grace is your escape from sin and self. It's God's tenacious love transforming ordinary you into an extraordinary reflection of your extraordinary Redeemer.

You're not the same today as you were yesterday, and you'll be different tomorrow – because grace is changing you.

Paradoxically, while grace is our peace and staying power – our *stickability* – on continents and in community, grace also unsticks us to move, obeying God's call. And grace unsticks in startling and subtle ways. Grace may move you to show up one more time for the friend who hasn't necessarily shown up for you.

God, mobilize me! Amen.

Both

Now may the God of peace make you holy in every way, and may your whole spirit and soul and body be kept blameless until our Lord Jesus Christ comes again. (1 Thess. 5:23 NLT)

Flying in an airplane is way different from flying in a spaceship – because of gravity. Your food doesn't fly off your plastic tray in an airplane and your feet are firmly on the floor. Even though you're actually suspended midair.

Our salvation is kind of like that. We're in a both-and – now-and-not-yet – space of traveling through time. At the moment of our salvation we were justified and at the moment of our death we'll be glorified. But everything in between is our daily sanctification by the Holy Spirit, and for that we depend on Someone other than ourselves to keep us grounded at the foot of the cross, and suspended by grace.

We're all somewhere between grace and gravity, dependent on both for stability, and mobility.

Jesus, thank You that my future is already settled and secure – even as You continue to reveal it in me bit by bit. Amen.

Quit hustling

I have been crucified with Christ and I no longer live, but Christ lives in me. The life I now live in the body, I live by faith in the Son of God, who loved me and gave Himself for me. (Gal. 2:20 NIV)

It may feel as if everyone's getting ahead of you. Take heart. Your agenda died with Christ. Thank God and good riddance. Relax now. His ways are so much better than any two-dimensional idea you can dream up.

God reaches down and delivers His best plans for your life, in the time and place He has you. Don't give in to the temptation to create a tall poppy culture – lopping off the blooms of those who rise higher than you.

Celebrate their wins the way you'd want them to celebrate yours. For all you know, they're looking at your life with the same sense of longing. Celebrate what God is growing in lives all around you – and in yours.

God, I don't want to exhaust myself chasing second-best stuff. Help me channel my energy into Your purposes for me. Amen.

Underneath

The eternal God is your refuge, and underneath are the everlasting arms. (Deut. 33:27 NIV)

Maybe you always felt like a hassle – an annoyance, a let-down or an embarrassment? So much so that now it's hard to accept people's friendship. You can't believe people actually like you. Maybe you grew up feeling you were too loud, or too quiet. Maybe you've been emotionally, verbally or physically abused, or you carry financial insecurity – a poverty mindset you're battling to think yourself out of.

No matter what your area of insecurity, or mine, it's always rooted in fear. Fear of failure, rejection, pain, lack, being out of the loop and so many other worries. A wise teacher said, "All fear is but the notion that God's love ends." What are you really afraid of? If you knew that God's everlasting love completely surrounded you behind and before, and that underneath were the everlasting arms – would it matter – the thing you fear? Perfect love casts out fear. And our perfect Savior loves you perfectly.

Lord, I'm calmed and comforted,
because Your love is much, much bigger
than my biggest fear. Amen.

Unlikely grace

Satisfy us each morning with Your unfailing love, so we may sing for joy to the end of our lives. (Ps. 90:14 NLT)

There are moments of unlikely grace all around us if we make even a small effort to notice them.

Walking past a construction site once, I glanced down at some building rubble – where a mommy mouse had made a safe, snug, happy nest amidst broken concrete, for her baby mice. *Unlikely grace.*

My boys tried to grow a lemon tree from seed in cotton wool. They figured it hadn't worked and tossed the seed into the garden – where it began to grow, and is still growing. *Unlikely grace.*

It's often in the unlikely places of life that beauty and grace show up. God makes ways where there seem to be none. He gives us the grace to adapt and make the best of the places we find ourselves in. He even refreshes our capacity to extend grace to others, reminding us that grace is about being positioned to reflect Jesus.

God, You've infused the universe
with unlikely grace. I'm amazed! Amen.

Big little world

He is my loving ally and my fortress, my tower of safety, my rescuer. He is my shield, and I take refuge in Him ... (Ps. 144:2 NLT)

No one can see us from space. Our existence is miniscule. We're just one of seven billion tiny human specks. Our stories don't occupy tremendous tracts of history.

And yet from across the universe and where you find yourself in this very moment, God hears the beats of your heart. No detail escapes Him.

He cares about and He uses the smallest, most seemingly insignificant interactions and events that populate our days. He holds all the big things and the little things in the palms of His hands and He wastes nothing, using even the tiny things we bring for enormous, eternal purpose.

When the mess of life threatens to overwhelm you – zoom out and get perspective, knowing that the Creator God is even now zooming in to bring you His peace.

Eternal God, thank You
for holding the universe,
and my hand. Amen.

Ground friendship

A friend loves at all times ... (Prov. 17:17 NIV)

Quite a while back, #FixWhatsBrokenIn5Words was trending on Twitter. It got me thinking that lasting change happens when we fix in our circle of influence, instead of ranting in our circle of concern. And really, our greatest influence rests in relationships.

Because of the supernatural inside-time-outside-time-all-the-time relevance of God's Holy Word, this five-word generating hashtag has been trending in the Bible for millennia. Take for example, *Friends love at all times* (Prov. 17:17). *Rejoice with those who rejoice. Weep with those who weep* (Rom. 12:15).

Here are some others we could try: *Show an interest; ask questions. Show grace to oversensitive friends. Show grace to insensitive friends. Listen, listen, listen. Then, listen. Don't be cliquey; it's ugly. Don't keep score; it's childish. Don't play the guilt card. Keeping in touch takes effort. Laugh as much as possible.*

Father, fix my broken bits so I can
be a safe, loyal, loving friend –
gracious, and grounding. Amen.

Be the green

"Your love for one another will prove to the world that you are My disciples." (John 13:35 NLT)

We've got a gray-water system in our garden, which means our lawn stays more or less green even when everything else is still dry, thirsty for summer. It reminds me that there's (metaphorical) brown grass all over the world. There isn't a patch of planet free from sleaze, prejudice or the odd suicide bomber.

The jury might still be out when it comes to the future of your country and the world. But I know I also need to admit that wherever I go in the world, I take myself with me. There's no getting away from me when I up and go off green-grass hunting.

Where there's green grass in the world, it's only because the people right there on that grass are watering it. If I'm not given to watering my grass right where I'm standing – what makes me think I'll bother to water it somewhere else?

God, help me to be for others the green grass I wish to walk on. Amen.

Grassroots grace

"And His name will be the hope of all the world." (Matt. 12:21 NLT)

What if we decided to get to the root of things? What if we stopped putting our hope in the lawn dressing and the topsoil? What if, right where we're standing, we let God drill holes in us – in our fears and in our comfort zones – so that He can spill out to make the grass green? What if we did everything in our power, with all the resources available to us, in the time we have left, right where God has us?

Let's determine that, today and forever, our hope is in Jesus Christ. This means being mobilized from self-preservation to self-sacrifice – compelled to love the world from the grass beneath our feet.

What if we welcomed the uncomfortable work of God in us – at grassroots level – and let the Living Water run right out of us, right where we are? I think it would change us. It might even change the world.

God, help me water the world,
where I'm standing. Amen.

Life laid down

Husbands, love your wives, just as Christ loved the church and gave Himself up for her. (Eph. 5:25 NIV)

If your husband is following his calling, then he'll love you like Christ loved the church. He'll lay down his life for you. That's way harder, way cooler, way sexier than submission. You need not be threatened by that kind of love. Except, maybe you're thinking, *Easy for you to say. You obviously have a really nice husband. You have no idea the kind of husband I'm dealing with.*

I would *never* assume to minimize your pain or disappointment. But hear this: even if your husband isn't willing to lay down his life for you, *Jesus Christ already has.* Jesus *already has* laid down His life for you, and therein lies your security.

At the cross, Jesus Christ took your shame, and restored your dignity. He's clothed you in righteous robes. Adopted you as a daughter. Gifted you with worth. That gift can't be taken away from you.

Jesus, thank You for how completely and utterly You demonstrate Your love for me. Amen.

Introvert grace

But Jesus often withdrew to
lonely places and prayed. (Luke 5:16 NIV)

Apparently 42% of humans are introverts. The rest are mostly extroverts. Some are ambiverts (that's me) with one foot in the still waters of introversion and the other kicking cheerfully in the public swimming pool with all the other extroverts.

If you're an introvert, there are things you should understand about how humans run the world. The loudest voices dominate the most important conversations. From social media to Starbucks, from schools to malls to movies – extroversion is held up as the ideal.

All this is totally fine. So long as you know that the world desperately needs leaders and creatives, and they need solitude and space. The most remarkable Leader and Creative ever, drew away to quiet spaces to pray. There's enough room inside your skin for you to feel completely comfortable. When you realize this, strength and peace are yours.

God, help me to go quietly inside
myself, with You. Amen.

Satisfied

So if we have enough food and clothing,
let us be content. (1 Tim. 6:8 NLT)

Trust God for grace so at the end of the day, when all your get-up-and-go has already got up and left, there's something – miraculously! – left of you. Something that remembers you and your people are on the same team. Something smiling and spontaneous.

Trust God for contentment. Because content is what you can be if you have food and clothing, and chances are you and I have too much of both. Trust God to reveal Himself to you today in such a way that you'll know that everything's going to be alright in the end. Maybe soon. Maybe much later. But definitely, alright in the end.

Ask God to let contentment settle deep in your bones so that if wish-dreams don't come true, you'll still be comfortably, happily sure that He'll bring you to the fullness He's planned and that your wise, well-resourced, loving God will lead you into all the good works prepared for you.

God, thanks to You, I'm happy right here
right now: content despite the crazy. Amen.

Perspective

"There is hope for your future,"
says the LORD. (Jer. 31:17 NLT)

Today, ask God to give you perspective, so you can rest in the truth that the earth is His, and everything in it (Ps. 24:1). That includes your family, wherever He's stuck you by grace and gravity to this planet.

Trust God for perspective on your home, so you'll remember that it will never be perfect, because humans live there. But it can be happy – crammed floor-to-ceiling with love. That way, you'll ease up on trying to fix everything and everyone.

Trust the Father for perspective so that you don't awfulize and catastrophize the future. Rather, you can make it your daily habit to actualize and normalize, hope and pray.

And ask God to restore your sense of humor. Chill out. Laugh at fun stuff and mostly at yourself. Thank God that He has Emmanuel – God with us all – the heart-link and lightness of being between us and our people.

God, help me remember that with Your strength
and wisdom, I can climb these mountains,
instead of trying to carry them. Amen.

Not here

"Why are you looking among the dead for someone who is alive? He isn't here! He is risen from the dead!" (Luke 24:5-6 NLT)

When Jesus-loving women rushed to the Savior's tomb in Jerusalem, the angel who greeted them told them He wasn't there. He'd risen. Jesus defied gravity and the grave – conquering death to rise again. And because of that, He extends His grace to us – His forgiveness and the gift of eternal, gravity-defying brand-new life with Him.

Imagine if we lived the truth Paul proclaims in Galatians 2:20. Imagine we lived as if our old self really had died – and been raised with Christ. Then, if sin came knocking, the internal soul-dialogue would go something like, "Sorry, she's not here. She's *risen*. You can't tempt her! She won't do that stuff anymore – the stuff her old (dead) self used to do. Her new living self? She's just not into that."

Jesus, thank You for conquering death, so I can really live! Show me where I'm still lugging a corpse. Help me to shake it off – my old dead self – and enjoy a risen life with You. Amen.

Inviting extraordinary

The reward for humility and fear of the LORD
is riches and honor and life. (Prov. 22:4 ESV)

I do not believe that I have ever met someone who wanted to be mediocre. Make no mistake – we're all just very ordinary humans. Yet we serve an extraordinary God who calls us to be extraordinary reflections of Him – extraordinary conduits of His glory. There's something of the image of God in each of us ordinary humans that is drawn to the *extraordinary*.

The world punts ideas of how we can get to extraordinary: the hustle of self-promotion and money and beauty and who-you-know. The Father's idea of extraordinary is counter-culture. I heard a preacher say once that humility is always an invitation for God to do extraordinary things.

As Jesus-followers, let's build our reputations on deference and happy self-denial. Let us invite our extraordinary God to do something extraordinary with our ordinary lives, by living lower.

God, from down here on my knees,
I'm asking You to come into my life
and do something remarkable,
for Your greatness and glory. Amen.

Rich man's world

For the love of money is the root of all kinds of evil. (1 Tim. 6:10 NLT)

The world is obsessed with money. And yet, money isn't wicked. It's like food, sex or speed or almost any other force or principle in existence: it can be used for tremendous good, and tremendous evil.

We need to hold our money lightly, aware that it's the *love* of money that is the root of evil, and aware that we can't even bank on money in the bank, because our money can be taken from us at any time. Money isn't who we are – and so more money doesn't make us better. More money is simply a tool to make better, wiser choices, and more money comes with even more responsibility.

Carry it carefully. And let go of it generously. In a rich man's world that lusts for stuff, our excellent stewardship and our generous giving are remarkable evidence of the work of the Holy Spirit in our hearts.

God, help me to unlove my money,
and shock the world! Amen.

Disproportionate

Yes, you will be enriched in every way so that you can always be generous. (2 Cor. 9:11 NLT)

It's been said that CEOs of the top five global fashion brands make in just four days what garment workers in Bangladesh earn over a lifetime. That kind of gross disparity shows there's something very wrong with the world's economic distribution.

The Father owns and distributes the wealth of the universe as He sees fit. He bestows riches on some and not on others. But this doesn't give us license to hoard our resources and clutch the good things He's given us. The Messiah who said we'd always have the poor with us also said that in giving generously to the needy, we're giving to Him.

If you're reading this book, I'm guessing you're literate, and you've likely been introduced to Jesus. That makes you more privileged than most people on the planet. Overwhelming gratitude for that reality should spill over into generosity.

Lord, You know my bank balance. Make me brave, wise and generous to use it, so that someone else can know You. Amen.

Feelings on a shoestring

"Blessed are the merciful ..." (Matt. 5:7 NIV)

I really like other humans. But occasionally my life collides with someone who hurts or angers me. Or knocks me off balance in some subtle way.

And sometimes I don't have it in me to muster the inner niceness, which is when I loan love from Jesus who feels all the feelings for all the people, and even feels them for me.

In moments when it's all I can do not to stoop and pick up an offence – because I'm irritated, insulted, threatened or hormonal – I say, *Jesus, can I use Your feelings right now? Help me feel for these people what You feel for them.*

Wearing Jesus' feelings thaws our icy agendas. There's real joy, real peace, real love. It's impossible to disdain or feel superior when you're warmed by the thought that Jesus had this person in mind when He hung on the cross.

Jesus, my heart's freezing.
Please loan me the warmth
of Your love. Amen.

Recline

And as Jesus reclined at table in the house, behold, many tax collectors and sinners came and were reclining with Jesus and His disciples. (Matt. 9:10 ESV)

What I've often missed when reading this story is how Jesus was reclining with His disciples as He spoke to the sinners and tax collectors who needed to hear His words.

Apparently, the Pharisees and other religious leaders of the day would never have dared to recline while talking about the Father. They always stood, as a sign of their power and authority. And yet Jesus reclined. He happily positioned Himself to be approachable. He humbled Himself – Creator-King – so that those who were still His enemies would feel safe in His presence.

Perhaps as we travel through life – acknowledging unreservedly that it's all about Him – we can find the time and space to recline. We can be amenable and accessible, welcoming others with a posture of humility.

Jesus, teach me Your ways of flexibility and friendliness, so I can win others over to Your remarkable love. Amen.

Not all fun

This is why we work hard and continue to struggle, for our hope is in the living God ... (1 Tim. 4:10 NLT)

Culture spins the feel-good philosophy that we should just chase our dreams. I believe God's calling on your life will have loads to do with where your passion and aptitude collide. Where you're good at doing something that you also love.

It's important to accept that leaning into the things you're passionate about – following your dreams – doesn't mean you only get to do the fun stuff. It's tough to read for the degree that fascinates you. But in the long hours of disciplined study there will be a quickening of the spirit that opting for fun or easy won't deliver.

Paul had an overriding passion to see the spread of the gospel across the world and this was the long-term achievement of his life. But his years were littered with hardships – as a result of that same passion. I think he'd be the first to say he wouldn't have chosen differently.

God, I'm weak, but I'm willing.
Let's do this thing. Amen.

Muscle memory

So I run with purpose in every step. I am not just shadowboxing. I discipline my body like an athlete, training it to do what it should. (1 Cor. 9:26-27 NLT)

Part of what helps us to go the distance and finish strong this side of eternity is the spiritual muscle memory we develop through every hardship we surrender to the power of God. We can trust Him to do in us what we can't do ourselves.

We can trust Him for wisdom and strength and insight, growth and endurance. If we make Jesus our training partner through trials, we build up residual courage which stands us in good stead when it comes to our future responses.

You can probably look back on your life and see where and how the Father was stockpiling your courage reserves – teaching and maturing you so that down the line you'd be able to cope better. And if you're currently facing overwhelming odds, trust God not to waste this experience. Ask Him to use it to strengthen sinews of wisdom and bravery, so you're well prepared for whatever you'll come across on the road ahead.

God, please don't waste anything that happens to me. Use it all to get me fit and strong for the stretch of road ahead. Amen.

Weights

You say, "I am allowed to do anything" – but not everything is good for you. You say, "I am allowed to do anything" – but not everything is beneficial. (1 Cor. 10:23 NLT)

If we're going to go the distance, we have to throw off the heavy things that have us dragging our feet. Maybe the weight you carry is the need to prove a point. Cast off that weight by occasionally keeping your opinions to yourself. Let's build up, not tear down.

Then there are the weights of comparison and staying angry and social media addiction and eating too much. Be honest with God and yourself about the things you need to drop.

Maybe you're too focused on carrying equally weighted dumbbells in each hand – living a balanced life. It's been said that no one living a balanced life ever changed the world. It's possible we'd be more striking in our Christ-likeness if we focused less on finding balance, and more on bearing fruit.

God, please show me what I need to drop,
so I can stay strong and go far. Amen.

Loving and leading

Children, always obey your parents. Fathers, do not aggravate your children, or they will become discouraged. (Col. 3:20-21 NLT)

We've blown it with our kids countless times, and doubtless we'll blow it countless more. But two things you and I should want our kids to know in the marrow of their bones, despite what we may or may not get right or wrong:

We are resolutely committed to loving them. We'll leverage all we are for all they're becoming. They are well loved, and loved well.

And we are passionately resolved to call out the potential God has placed in them. We should want our kids to be the best possible versions of themselves and leave the planet better than they found it.

Part of that potential is to lead, because we're all called to lead our own lives, and lead others to Christ. Also, it's exactly in uncertain times (now!) that the world needs the clear vision of tenacious leaders.

Father, as a parent I can't tick all the boxes all the time. Help me to simply love and lead my kids, so we can go the distance. Amen.

Currents

I will refuse to look at anything vile and vulgar. (Ps. 101:3 NLT)

A received an email explaining: "I find it very disturbing how it's so hard to find a movie or series to watch that isn't full of sickeningly gross violence or sexual depravity or messed up twisted concepts. It bothers me that believers find it ok to fill their minds with such horrible things and even worse, *enjoy* it. How do we as Christians deal with this as well as keep our children safe from numbing their minds to such terrible things?"

To go the distance – to finish well without getting sidetracked by the real evil described above (because haven't we all struggled with various degrees of entertainment-related guilt, frustration and disgust?) – let's admit that the undertow of cultural currents will take us to dark places.

It'll be hard work – swimming upstream – but it'll make you fitter and stronger than those drifting downstream. Let's keep searching for something wholesome to watch. Read. Talk. Hug each other. We'll be glad we did.

Jesus, make me immovable on my resolve to keep it clean. Amen.

Grit and grace

Work hard to show the results of your salvation, obeying God with deep reverence and fear. (Phil. 2:12 NLT)

Jesus came to earth as one hundred percent God and one hundred percent man. I've come to accept this *both-and* reality as one of the beautiful God-mysteries permeating the universe. Something similar happens in us. Much of life is walking the tightrope of grit and grace – working as if it's one hundred percent up to us, and praying as if it's one hundred percent up to God.

He lends us every breath and infuses our muscles and brain cells with energy and potential: without Him we are nothing, and we can do nothing. And yet concurrently He holds us accountable to decide to use our gifts and opportunities – our money, time, abilities and relationships – for His Kingdom and glory.

And there's nothing quite like the exhausted satisfaction of accomplishment: knowing that you gave it your absolute human best, and that the Father was supernaturally empowering you.

Jesus, help me harness every fiber of my potential even as I depend fully on You. Amen.

Spiders

Who will free me from this life that is dominated by sin and death? Thank God! The answer is in Jesus Christ our Lord ... (Rom. 7:24-25 NLT)

There is no denying we all have besetting sins that repeatedly trip us up. It might be substance abuse or gossip. Overspending or overeating. Envy or materialism or lust or irresponsible escapism. Maybe you've tried to deal with your sin. You have prayed and repented. You've memorized Scripture, read books, gone for counseling.

Those are all good things to do. Keep doing them. But Carlos Whitaker suggests there's no point continually cleaning out the cobwebs – sweeping out the corners of your mind where a tangled transgression mesh collects. *You have to kill the spider* – or it'll keep spinning its webs of sin.

Perhaps the spider is fear or pride or the lie you've believed about yourself. Perhaps you're really assailed by debilitating insecurity and that is what has you lashing out in all sorts of hurtful ways. Ask God to show you the spider. Waste no time. Kill it.

Lord, give me a holy arachnophobia.
Exterminate whatever's spinning
webs to snare me. Amen.

All sides

... He faced all of the same testings we do,
yet He did not sin. (Heb. 4:15 NLT)

If we are going to finish strong, we need to be intentional about how we carry and cover ourselves. To live wholeheartedly, soft-science researchers suggest we need to have a strong back, a soft front, and a heroic heart. That means, marshaling the courage to stand up for ourselves and for others and for the truth; being vulnerable; and borrowing all the inner brave we need from our soft, strong Savior.

Ask God to show you if any of those three things is lacking in your life. Is your heart soft and open to those around you – but you're too easily manipulated or mismanaged? Or are you relentlessly courageous and principled – without the compassion necessary to temper your stance?

Not one of us will ever be perfectly brave or perfectly loving – but the Holy Spirit transforms us more and more into the likeness of perfectly brave, perfectly loving Jesus.

Jesus, You lived perfectly, and You
perfectly understand my imperfection.
Make me both supple and sturdy on all
sides – built for brave. Amen.

Shovel coal

Whoever pursues righteousness and unfailing love will find life, righteousness, and honor. (Prov. 21:21 NLT)

We have all seen Christian leaders going strong for a while – then flaking out of a failing ministry. We've all seen Christian leaders who get wiser and godlier. Why and how do some go the distance, and others not?

A steam train keeps going for miles after its engine has cut out. People are the same. If we stop shoveling the coal of prayer, truth, fellowship and accountability, we can keep going for quite some time. But eventually the impetus peters out.

An older, wiser man of God said to me once that to go the distance, "do God's bidding for your life. Do it resolutely, humbly, no matter the cost." That translates into our lives as: daily time with God; journaling our prayers and convictions; not Band-Aiding the heart-sepsis of sin; and remembering that our Father sees and rewards every small act of obedience to the Spirit's prompting. Keep refueling your resolve to go the distance.

God, don't let me cruise through life on momentum. Help me travel well by daily leaning on and learning from You. Amen.

Heights

The Sovereign LORD is my strength! He makes me as surefooted as a deer, able to tread upon the heights. (Hab. 3:19 NLT)

As you continue to go the distance in this life – heading for heaven – there will no doubt be valleys and sheer cliffs – some harsh, some beautiful. Success can have you standing on heights with magnificent views – and adverse circumstances or your own sin can have you standing on scary, slippery heights. In every case, God is able to make you stand on those heights.

Whatever breathtaking, exhilarating altitude you reach, or whatever pinnacle of pain you find yourself standing on, God will have the final say in your life. Not circumstances. Not another person. Not your success. Not even your sin.

All those things might be impacting you, but they can't define your destiny, because God is sovereign even over our waywardness and His purposes cannot be thwarted (Job 42:2).

Yahweh, thank You that no matter what precarious place I find myself teetering on the edge of – I needn't crouch and cling all alone. You are with me, and You make me able to stand. Amen.

Daughters

God decided in advance to adopt us into
His own family by bringing us to Himself
through Jesus Christ. (Eph. 1:5 NLT)

It's unlikely that a child abandoned on the streets will amount to much. But a child adopted – cherished and nurtured in a home where she belongs and is beloved – will flourish.

You are not abandoned, and never will be. You're adopted. More than that, you are adopted by a loving King – which makes you royalty. And even more than that – you're adopted by the King who signed the papers for your adoption with His own blood, securing your belonging for eternity.

Why then, do you and I still sometimes behave as if we're scraping together an existence on the streets outside the palace – as if we haven't been invited in, clothed, given our own room and a place at the table?

You're a daughter in the house – warm, clothed and fed – and your wise, excellent, loving Father will give you all you need.

Father, thank You for calling me into Your
courts so that I'm equipped to go back out
into the streets, carrying Your name. Amen.

Live like it's new

Place me like a seal over your heart,
like a seal on your arm. (Song 8:6 NLT)

For your marriage to go the distance, you sometimes have to pretend you're just starting out. So, if you're newly married, *do fun stuff*! And if you've been married for eons, pretend you're newly married, and *do fun stuff*!

Don't constantly host hordes of people in your home – at the expense of your alone time. Switch off your phones sometimes and savor the ultimate, intimate *us*-factor of being newlyweds – or even better, *experienced* weds.

Find excuses to celebrate anything, like the fact that it's Tuesday. Go out, go away, stay home, be alone. *Plan* for spontaneity. Scheduled romance is better than no romance. Always have something to look forward to.

And make a lot of love. He might need it more. You might need it less. That's just how God made us. Do the dance of compromise and compassion and lay yourselves down for each other's needs.

God, whether our marriage is
brand new or worn in, help us live it all
like it's the first time. Amen.

Not the man you married

Always be humble and gentle. Be patient with each other, making allowance for each other's faults because of your love. (Eph. 4:2 NLT)

You'll hear women say, "But he's not the man I married!" He shouldn't be. If he's exactly the same as he was on your wedding day, he hasn't grown at all.

That said, don't start living separate lives. Keep finding each other. Talk for long enough to get to the laughing part. Behave more like his lover and less like his mother. Fight to uncover and rediscover each other's sense of humor and hope.

Don't humiliate each other, and don't enable each other. In a good marriage, you know each other so well that you can start compensating for each other's weaknesses to the point that there's resentment or an unhealthy shift in responsibilities. Don't stop challenging each other and calling each other out on stuff. You're life partners, not co-dependents.

Your stress will affect him, and his stress will affect you. Again, the whole one-flesh thing. Remember: us against the problem.

God, keep us doing all we can to help each other go further. Amen.

Old people have it going on

The way of the righteous is like the first gleam of dawn, which shines ever brighter until the full light of day. (Prov. 4:18 NLT)

I once spoke to folks in their late-eighties and nineties. They had chesty coughs and all the other things that go with decades of earthly wear-and-tear. And they were a far greater inspiration to me than I was to them.

It's tempting to feel superior to the old because from the outside, their worlds have shrunk. Yet we'd be fools to dismiss them, because on the inside their lives have turned big. Their worlds have expanded – so much so that they're almost touching eternity. Their time isn't running out; it's running *towards*.

They bruise dark from every bump and maybe it's because they've lived long enough to know real compassion – to feel the world's pain with readiness to bleed for it – like Jesus. Maybe their paper-thin skin is evidence of the thin places they live – where heaven meets earth. It's possible that, really, this is their finest hour.

God, I want to age exquisitely,
to glorify You. Amen.

Words that go the distance

Take control of what I say, O Lord,
and guard my lips. (Ps. 141:3 NLT)

We're shaped by the language we use, and if we want to go the distance for God it's crucial that we exercise verbal precision – as opposed to verbosity or exaggeration. Because surely God is strong enough through us, with the actual truth. We don't need to inflate it or embellish it.

This challenge is not just for writers or speakers or teachers or radio presenters. We all use words every day, and God will ask us to give an account of each one (Matt. 12:36). Let's travel light by offloading a bunch of unnecessary words. Ill-timed conversations. Gossip, slander and any other maliciousness. God's Word has gone the distance through all of human history, so His words are a good place to start if we're wondering how to shape our own.

Creator of communication, choose the words I send out into the world today. Let whatever comes out of me be wise, life-giving, timely and true. Amen.

Off the map, into the mire

I trust in God, so why should I be afraid? What can mere mortals do to me? (Ps. 56:4 NLT)

It's no exaggeration that we're traveling into difficult days. Every media stream broadcasts how the world has gone all sorts of senseless and it's going to take a fight for us not to lose our joy in these dark days.

It's a fight worth fighting because it sets us apart as believers. The world should watch our lives and go, "There's something weird – and compelling – about those Jesus people. They're in serious trouble. It looks like they're in quicksand like the rest of us. They seem to have lost their maps in the mud – *but they haven't lost their hope.*"

Perhaps the greatest gift we can give to the next generation is not to let these complicated times – politically, economically, ideologically or culturally – mar our children. We could let our kids and others see that they needn't fear death. Also, they needn't fear life.

God, even as the mud squelches between
my toes, I'm declaring that You are
my joy for the journey. Amen.

Grounded for change

My heart is steadfast, O God! I will sing and make melody with all my being! (Ps. 108:1 ESV)

The whole point of our existence is to change – to become more like Jesus – so change isn't something we should fear. We live for the changeless God who changes us.

So we need to accept and assume that God will call us to walk off the map. We will know failure and weakness and surprise attacks. He will challenge our thinking, our attitudes and actions. We'll feel the tremors of revolution and He'll lend us the wisdom to measure them and investigate their source. It's ok – in fact it's expected of us – to be curious and open to how life around us is advancing. We can accept, embrace and welcome transformation.

So long as we're grounded.

Let's study the Scriptures so we'll know the truth. It will set us free. Let's be still, so we'll recognize the unchanging voice of our Heavenly Father, even when all around us is changing.

Lord, tie me to Your truth,
so I'm free to travel. Amen.

Always afloat

" ... upon this rock I will build My church, and all the powers of hell will not conquer it." (Matt. 16:18 NLT)

Living life for Jesus can seem risky. If we look at our lives the way others might – others who don't know and trust and believe Jesus the way we do – it can seem like we've lost the plot. Like, why would we *give away* chunks of our income when times are tough? Why would we put ourselves in danger by traveling to hostile countries to tell people about God's love?

People might sneer that Christianity is a sinking ship – but it's simply not the truth. The storm is outside of our boat, not in it. God promises to provide and protect. He *made* the sea and He holds it together. If you're seeking Him first, you can sail any kind of sea, expectantly and with great peace.

Jesus endorsed His church, guaranteeing its survival and making it the only ship that comes with any kind of no-sinking guarantee.

Jesus, thank You for keeping me and every molecule and meteoroid, afloat. Amen.

Lost and found

"If you try to hang on to your life, you will lose it. But if you give up your life for My sake, you will save it." (Matt. 16:25 NLT)

Jesus asks us to lose our lives for His sake, and in so doing, we'll find *real* life – the abundant life He came to bring.

The life we're losing is the (false) sense of security we get from our stuff, our relationships, our economics, and all the other things onto which we can be tempted to fix our hope.

Losing our lives doesn't mean losing our way. Others might scoff that you've "found religion" and lost your way – that you need a real GPS to navigate the complexities of life. The liberating truth is that you can navigate just fine, because Jesus says, "I am the way, the truth, and the life" (John 14:6). He *is the way* – and you *know* Him – so you know the way. Follow the way, and you'll reach your destination.

Jesus, You don't just know
the route I should take.
You are the route I should take.
Thank You! Amen.

Off the map

Mark out a straight path for your feet so that those who are weak and lame will not fall but become strong. (Heb. 12:13-14 NLT)

To love the human race the way the Heavenly Father does and to navigate relationships excellently, we need to know that love is almost always inconvenient. Love will cost us time out of our hectic schedules. Love will cost us detours from our focused to-dos. Love will often cost us money.

But the cost is worth it because at the end of our lives how we treated others and managed our relationships is all that will really matter, and all that will really be remembered. And perhaps the closest thing to perfection this side of heaven is to love others well. We can do this by making a sincere effort to listen, and to translate our intentions into other people's realities.

It will take courage and conviction, but in traveling the bypasses of inconvenient love we'll happen upon beauty we wouldn't otherwise have seen.

God, show me who I need to love today, by walking off the map of my plans and preferences. Amen.

Dot to dot

Many are the plans in a person's heart,
but it is the LORD's purpose
that prevails. (Prov. 19:21 NIV)

We're all moving into an unknown future. None of us can see past the next five minutes – or indeed the next breath that the Heavenly Father lends us. It may feel pointless even having a map – making a plan – picking a route – because there are no guarantees and God alone knows where we're really going and how much time we have left.

Choose today to celebrate God's sovereignty, providence, love, wisdom and power. All of life's burning questions have actual answers, and God knows them. Praise Him that, sure, you don't have a clue what tomorrow will bring, but He does.

Thank Him that He's connecting the dots, all the time. Enjoy the truth that anywhere you go, you're sent. And as your dot-to-dot journey is disclosed – dot by God-ordained dot – you'll get to discover more of the mystery of His eternal kindness.

God, some days I really have
no idea where I'm going.
I'm so grateful that You do. Amen.

Daily future mercy

Great is His faithfulness; His mercies begin afresh each morning. (Lam. 3:23 NLT)

It's often easier to live with your own pain, than to watch a loved one living with theirs. If you look to the future and unrest tugs at your gut, perhaps it's because you can't imagine there's a hope and a future for your kids. It may seem as if they will certainly have to walk right off the known map, and not knowing what that will look like can be scary.

Take a deep breath, and take heart. The Father has promised that His grace is sufficient for the travels of each adult – each child – each grandchild (2 Cor. 12:9). He will make a way for *each one* – even when it seems the road runs out. His plans are perfect and He is perfectly powerful to fulfill them.

Almighty God, I'm grateful that, even if tougher times lie ahead, You're already in the future and You'll lend us and our kids capacity to carry whatever comes. Amen.

City peace

Work for the peace and prosperity of the city where I sent you into exile. Pray to the Lord for it, for its welfare will determine your welfare. (Jer. 29:7 NLT)

If the map of your life has taken you to – or left you in – a place you'd rather not be, pray for the welfare of the city you're in, because its welfare will affect your welfare. That's not to say you'll stay there forever. God may alleviate your angst by moving you somewhere more comfortable or more exciting.

But maybe He won't. Maybe God will get maximum glory from your life on earth by leaving you where you are. Pray that He would open your eyes to the beauty and opportunity that you've missed.

Pray that He would grow rich, ripe, low-slung fruit from your branches, and make you a place of shade and rest for the people around you. You never know: you may suddenly realize that you're unbelievably satisfied with the life you already have.

Lord, bless the streets and
the citizens surrounding me.
Make me an agent of peace
and productivity. Amen.

Way out

God is faithful. When you are tempted,
He will show you a way out so that
you can endure. (1 Cor. 10:13 NLT)

I have days that unravel. The fibers whiz loose from my happy mom ensemble. I'm stripped of kind composure and my kids are tripping over tangled heaps of angry words at my feet. There are loose threads lying ugly to end the day threadbare. How do I pick up dropped stitches and tie tight the slack strings with truth and love?

That's when I hear Paul's heartening reminder – that what I'm experiencing isn't different from what others go through. God won't push me beyond my limits, and He'll show me a way out.

God doesn't give us a loophole. He shows us a way out. Jesus said, "I am the way ..." (John 14:6). The way into the truth about how to do life and live it for the Father – He's right here with me in the mess. He is the way out, from the mess of me.

Jesus, You're the lit exit sign
from my sin and myself.
Thank You! Amen.

Find them

"For God so loved the world that He gave His one and only Son, that whoever believes in Him shall not perish but have eternal life." (John 3:16 NIV)

Most of the people who fill my days are fellow believers. I'm challenged by that. I don't have so many of the proverbial tax collectors and sinners coming over to our place.

And yet, if I'm not deeply burdened for the lost – *that's a problem*. While I can pray and trust God to bring people across my path, sometimes I have to *find* them.

Are you seeking out the lost? It might be horribly uncomfortable. You definitely won't always know what to say. But if you trust God for wisdom in the moment, you'll have it. And if you fear that your timing is off, know that it's always a good time to demonstrate the fruit of the Spirit (Gal. 5:22-23).

Love never fails, which means you can't possibly get it wrong. Start there.

Jesus, Mission Earth was to seek
and save the lost. Help me get
with the program! Amen.

Cheering

Be happy with those who
are happy ... (Rom. 12:15 NLT)

Perhaps "sky's the limit" is seriously not something you'd apply to celebrating the success of others. If you're honest – you're jealous. You're angry with God because He hasn't blessed you the way He's blessed your successful friend. Your sour grapes say that you don't believe God has it in Him to bless you in the same way.

Try telling yourself this truth: the sky's the limit when it comes to God's resources. He's your *Father*. Why would He not, *how could He not*, only ever have your ultimate wellbeing at heart, even if that ultimate wellbeing isn't what you had in mind?

Don't worry about what the Father is doing in other people's lives. Seek Him first, and seek first His Kingdom, and everything else will be added. Then enjoy making much of your successful friends, associates and family members, knowing that God will take full responsibility for the consequences at play in a life fully devoted to Him.

God, I know You can make a
cheerleader of me yet! Amen.

Heavenly minded

Point out anything in me that offends You,
and lead me along the path of
everlasting life. (Ps. 139:24 NLT)

People disdain Christians for being so heavenly minded they're of no earthly good. That's junk. If your mind is really set on eternity, you'll be a force for seismic change. Your priorities will shift and free you of negligible concerns. You'll be moved to speak hope in a world of broken bodies and shattered souls. And because you're fearfully and wonderfully made, God will use you in a distinct, remarkable way, according to your passions and opportunities, to take Kingdom ground, and change the world.

So to make a lasting difference? Embrace how the Heavenly Father has shaped you – your gifts; your physical, emotional and intellectual quirks; and your obvious shortcomings. Bow low before Him. Surrender your spiritual deficiencies to the scrutiny of the Spirit. As He convicts, forgives and restores, your life will be different. And so will the world.

Father, fix my heart on eternity,
so it helps me fix earth. Amen.